Teachers or Parents

Who is responsible for raising the next generation?

Teachers or Parents

Who is responsible for
raising the next generation?

Joanna Williams

CIVITAS

First Published
September 2024

© Civitas 2024
55 Tufton Street
London SW1P 3QL

email: books@civitas.org.uk

ISBN 978-1-912581-59-7

Independence: Civitas: Institute for the Study of Civil
Society is a registered educational charity (No. 1085494)
and a company limited by guarantee (No. 04023541).
Civitas is financed from a variety of private sources to
avoid over-reliance on any single or small group of donors.

All the Institute's publications seek to further its objective
of promoting the advancement of learning. The views
expressed are those of the authors, not of the Institute.

Typeset by Typetechnique

Printed in Great Britain by
4edge Limited, Essex

Contents

Author

Joanna Williams is an academic and author. She is the author of *How Woke Won* (2022); *Women vs Feminism* (2017); *Academic Freedom in an Age of Conformity* (2016); and *Consuming Higher Education: Why Learning Can't Be Bought* (2012). She is a columnist for *Spiked* and writes regularly for *The Times*, *The Spectator*, and *The Telegraph*.

Joanna began her career teaching English in secondary schools. She joined the University of Kent as lecturer in Higher Education and Academic Practice in 2007, where she later became director of the Centre for the Study of Higher Education. Since leaving academia in 2019, Joanna has worked for think tanks including Policy Exchange and the Centre for Independent Studies. Joanna's previous reports for Civitas include *Policing Hate*; *Rethinking Race: A Critique of Contemporary Anti-Racism* and *The Corrosive Impact of Transgender Ideology*. She is currently a visiting fellow at Mathias Corvinus Collegium in Budapest.

Foreword

This excellent and timely report articulates why the raising of children has become so highly contested in the United Kingdom.

It used to be widely accepted that parents had authority over their children. Mothers and fathers were responsible for their children's physical safety, for feeding, clothing, and sheltering their offspring, and raising them with a moral and spiritual foundation according to their own beliefs and traditions. Schools existed to teach children to read, write, and add up, and to impart the skills and knowledge that they would require for adult life.

Anyone who has set foot in a British secondary school recently will have observed that the remit of our education system has expanded far beyond teaching the 'three Rs'. From 'diversity week', assemblies encouraging climate action, or adverts for the lunchtime LGBTQ+ club, British schools have become increasingly concerned with promoting social action to children.

As the report attests, in addition to their academic responsibilities, schools have always played an important role in 'socialising' children to prepare them for adult life. We take for granted that through their school experience, children will learn important virtues and 'soft skills' such as patience, tolerance, hard work, self-control, and how to work collaboratively with others.

But as this report so clearly sets out, over the last decade or two there has been a concerning 'mission creep' in many schools: responsibility for socialising children has morphed into a determination to drive social, moral, and even sexual change, often against the wishes and values of parents and the wider public. Many parents are concerned that teachers are undermining their right to raise their children as they wish, and teachers feel unsupported in their role by parents.

These tensions will be familiar to anyone who has recent experience of education, and this report brilliantly articulates the cause of mutual distrust; namely that the boundaries between parents' rights and teachers' responsibility have become blurred. On the one hand, many parents are failing in their responsibilities, with alarming numbers of children starting school without being potty trained, and many are failing to instil in their children the standards of behaviour and respect for others that are necessary for school – and adult – life. On the other hand, many schools are encroaching on the authority of parents, from issuing patronising instructions about what to feed children or when to allow them to walk home from school alone, to serious and shocking instances of schools keeping secrets from parents about what children are being taught, or about their son's or daughter's decision to 'change gender'.

This blurring of boundaries between parents and schools is not a minor problem that can be muddled through; it is fundamentally undermining the collective authority of adults in Britain. When teachers tell children that parents who hold traditional views are bigoted, the authority of the parent is weakened. When parents criticise a child's teacher in their hearing, the authority of that teacher is weakened. Yet many parents now feel they have no choice but to warn their children that what they are told by their teachers about certain topics may in fact not be true. A whole generation of children is being deprived of the security of being able to trust those who care for them and of the certainty of knowing what is expected of them in adult life.

In addition to providing much-needed clarity about what has gone wrong and how, the report offers inspiration for where to go from here. Joanna Williams suggests we must be far clearer about the demarcation of responsibilities between school and home. We need a collective acknowledgement that 'the primary role of the school is the transmission of knowledge and the primary role of the family is nurturing children, including their moral and spiritual development'.

The challenge is going to be to persuade schools – and the government – to let go. To let go of the insistence that children need to be taught about contentious ideas in which schools are not expert and for which there is little evidence of benefit. And, apart from in extreme cases, schools will have to let go of taking responsibility for children whose parents are not fulfilling their duties. If schools continue to allow children to turn up in nappies, parents will continue to send them to school that way. We must understand that when responsibility is taken away from people, people become irresponsible.

There will be a period of pain as both parents and schools readjust. But readjust they must, because without the protective shield of collective adult authority, our children are far more vulnerable to both people and ideas that mean them harm. As Joanna Williams writes so compellingly, we don't want schools and families to be 'competitors' or even 'partners'; rather, parents and teachers should be firm 'allies' in the vital task of raising and socialising the next generation.

Miriam Cates
Former Member of Parliament for Penistone and Stocksbridge

Introduction

What happens in schools rarely stays within the classroom. Today, everything from the content of the curriculum, topics for assemblies, dress codes and behaviour policies, to the food served at lunchtime, is subject to public scrutiny. Sometimes individual schools are thrust into the spotlight. In February 2024, Michaela School in North London hit the headlines after prayer rituals were banned and a Muslim pupil sued for discrimination.[1] Sometimes one issue prompts national debate, such as how schools respond to children confused about their gender. Many of these disputes share a common cause: tension between the rights of parents and the responsibilities of teachers.

Schools and teaching unions berate parents for failing to prepare children for school. Recent complaints have focused upon children starting school still wearing nappies; parents sending children to school with poor quality lunches; children not knowing how to use a knife and fork; or how to behave appropriately in a classroom.[2] At the same time, parents express alarm about teachers overstepping their role. There was, until recently, significant concern at schools allowing children to change gender without their parents' knowledge;[3] using sexually inappropriate resources in Relationships and Sex Education classes;[4,5] and using the classroom to teach contested political ideas grounded in critical race theory or gender ideology.[6]

Once, the division of labour between school and home seemed clear. Parents were responsible for their children's physical, emotional and moral wellbeing while teachers were responsible for education. Yet, as we discuss in

Chapter Two, schools have always provided an element of moral instruction and socialisation alongside teaching subject knowledge. By the same token, in providing food at lunchtime and lessons in personal hygiene or domestic science, schools compensated for the presumed inadequacies of some homes. Informally, some teachers no doubt went further in giving food or clean clothes to disadvantaged pupils, just as some parents buy books, hire private tutors and encourage children in extra study. Such instances rarely trigger disputes within a context of broad agreement among adults about the values and attitudes to be instilled in children and a general consensus about the role each member of a community plays in helping to raise the next generation. This report explores how this consensus has broken down.

When the transmission of subject knowledge is no longer the primary goal of education, schools increasingly promote adherence to beliefs that are more overtly political in nature. Lessons about gender, sexuality and race can run directly counter to the views of parents. Rather than teachers and parents working towards shared goals, parents come to be considered an obstacle to children developing 'correct' moral and political values. This sets up hostility between school and home which can spill over into blame and, in extreme cases, protests outside school gates. Parents are deemed inadequate while teachers stand accused of interfering.

Disputes between school and home speak not just to a lack of clarity about what it means to raise the next generation but also to a profound lack of trust between adults in the present. As we argue throughout this report, disputes between teachers and parents undermine collective adult authority in the eyes of children and prompt a crisis in socialisation – the routine ways in which a new generation is introduced to the norms and values of the existing world. This has a detrimental impact on both education and home life. The crisis takes its clearest form in concerns over children's poor behaviour or young children starting school not fully toilet-trained. Although some of these issues may be overstated, press coverage indicates not just confusion about the differing roles of parents and teachers but a sense that at least some parents may have abdicated responsibility for key aspects of child rearing, safe in the knowledge that teachers will pick up the slack. In turn, as teachers dedicate more time to tasks previously left to parents, they have even less time to dedicate to education.

Here, we consider why there has been a blurring of the boundaries between school and home, what form this takes and what can be done to rescue both education and the paramountcy of the parent/child relationship.

1.

Current tensions between home and school

Certain aspects of home school relations are particularly controversial. Here, we explore the politicisation of education and the exploitation of the curriculum to inculcate in children values that may run directly counter to those of their family and community. Classes in Relationships and Sex Education provide the clearest example of schools moving away from teaching academic subject knowledge to instructing children in contested beliefs. Teachers further step into responsibilities traditionally assumed by parents with the expansion of the pastoral role to encompass a therapeutic focus on children's emotional regulation and mental health. At the same time, there is growing concern that some parents might be abdicating responsibility for ensuring their children arrive at school ready to learn, attend regularly and behave appropriately.

Together, these tensions speak to a shift in the role of teachers from experts in academic subjects to experts in childhood. Unable (or unwilling) to assume authority in the classroom on the basis of superior subject knowledge, teachers claim authority in relation to child development. This often takes a therapeutic focus on child mental health. In response, nervous about getting things wrong, or simply reassured that if they do not instruct their child then someone else will, some parents can appear to be abdicating tasks that were traditionally considered to be the responsibility of the family.

The politicisation of education

Education has become politicised in three key ways. First is the addition of new subjects into the school curriculum which are inherently political in nature. For example, Relationships and Sex Education lessons cover contested concepts like gender identity and the nature of intimate relationships while Citizenship classes look to cultivate particular attitudes to the nation and the environment. Second, more traditional academic subjects have introduced new content, such as geography which focuses on sustainability and environmentalism, literature which becomes a vehicle for exploring attitudes towards race and gender, or history which centres the sins of the nation state. Third, the messages pupils pick up outside of timetabled lessons through assemblies with guest speakers, charity days, the posters on display in school buildings and policies around behaviour and uniform. This 'extra' or 'hidden' curriculum has become fertile ground for activist-teachers.

Relationships and Sex Education

In May 2024, as one of its final acts in office, the Conservative government announced new guidance for the teaching of Relationships and Sex Education. Children were not to be taught about sex before the age of nine and contested ideas about gender identity were not to be taught as facts.[7] This was an important step towards altering a curriculum that had come to be perceived as overly sexualised and highly politicised. In order to appreciate the concerns of parents, and the lack of trust some have for teachers, we need to consider what schools were offering children prior to this intervention which, as of July 2024, may yet be rescinded by the newly elected Labour government.

Previous statutory guidance on Relationships and Sex

Education had been introduced in 2019 and came into effect in 2021. Backed by Theresa May and implemented under Boris Johnson's premiership, the new curriculum was influenced by groups like Stonewall as well as international organisations such as the World Health Organization and UNESCO that promoted a shift from sex to sexuality education.[8] What this means is that rather than just teaching the basic facts of life, classes in secondary schools were to cover topics such as 'consent, sexual exploitation, online abuse, grooming, coercion, harassment, rape, domestic abuse, forced marriage, honour-based violence and FGM'.[9] In addition, schools were to teach children about gender identity and same-sex relationships. Children were taught not to assume that cis-gendered people, heterosexual relationships or the traditional family are, in any way, 'normal'.

Significantly, while parents maintained the right to withdraw their children from sex education, they could not remove them from relationships classes. This not only made attendance in the most overtly politicised and contested lessons compulsory, it also effectively nulled the right to withdraw children from sex education classes. When pupils looked at their school timetables, they saw RSE as a single subject. Withdrawing children from sex education while ensuring they attended mandatory relationships lessons would have required them to enter and leave a classroom at five-minute intervals.

In June 2023, mother Clare Page lost her legal case to access the teaching materials used in her daughter's school's Relationships and Sex Education lessons. Her campaign to view the lesson plans and resources began in 2021, after her daughter returned from school saying that she had been taught to be 'sex positive' and that heteronormativity was 'a bad thing'. Page discovered that the school, along with around 300 others, was using resources provided by the School of Sexuality Education. Page submitted Freedom of Information requests to try to see the material but the School of Sexuality Education refused to publish its lesson plans. It was backed by the Information Commissioner's Office which argued that the charity's commercial interest in keeping its resources private outweighed the public interest in publishing them. Page appealed but a first-tier tribunal upheld the ICO's judgement.[10] However, government guidance issued in May 2024 sought to clarify parents' right to know what their children are being taught in RSE. It was also noted that parents can request to see teaching materials.[11]

This legal case came amid heightened concern that children were being routinely subjected to sexually explicit material in Relationships and Sex Education lessons that were ideologically-driven, scientifically inaccurate, sexualised children at an inappropriately young age and did so without parental knowledge or consent. The research group New Social Covenant Unit published a dossier of evidence setting out the content of so-called 'sex positive' classes.[12] They highlighted classroom activities that involve children 'stepping away from heteronormative and monogamy-based assumptions' in order to appreciate that 'there are a variety of sexual preferences and practices – we're all a little different'. This could involve children being taught about topics such as masturbation, oral sex, anal sex, fisting, rough sex, gender queer or polyamory with the youngest children expected to engage in activities such as drawing penises and making vulvas out of Play-Doh.[13]

In October 2023, Education Secretary Gillian Keegan wrote to all schools in England to clarify that: 'Parents should be able to see what their children are being taught in RSHE lessons. Schools must share teaching materials with parents.'[14] This did little to alter the balance of power between school and home when it came to teaching children about relationships. Despite parents, journalists, think tanks and MPs all having raised concerns about sexually graphic and age-inappropriate content being routinely used in school sex-education classes, as we have previously noted, another round of guidance was required in Spring 2024.

Relationships and Sex Education is not a traditional school subject. It has no disciplinary basis, no substantive body of knowledge and – although some make claims to the contrary – there is no such thing as a relationships 'expert'. Relationships and Sex Education is a means of imparting a pre-determined set of moral values and political assumptions to school pupils who comprise a captive audience in the classroom. Although lessons may now have changed, subject to further reviews by the Labour government, the previous iteration of RSE caused harm. It did harm to individual pupils who were subjected to inappropriate content that encouraged some to question their own gender identity and perhaps even seek medical interventions. But there was also harm to collective parental authority in promoting the idea that the state, via teachers, is responsible for imparting attitudes and values about the most intimate aspects of life.[15]

Citizenship education
Citizenship education is another example of a political project that has been transformed into a school subject. Its place on the school curriculum reflects efforts at steering children away from more organic associations with national identity; classes aim at re-directing children towards social justice, sustainability and loyalty to transnational institutions. Citizenship classes often promote community

activism as the primary form of democratic engagement and the values of global, rather than national, citizenship.

Citizenship education took off under the 1997 New Labour government amid growing concern with social exclusion and young people who did not vote or otherwise engage with public institutions. An Advisory Group on Citizenship and Democracy in Schools was established, chaired by Professor Bernard Crick, and the group's final report was published in 1998. The ambitious aim was, 'no less than a change in the political culture of this country both nationally and locally'.[16] The report argued that all children needed citizenship lessons to tackle 'political disconnection'.

In August 2002, the Labour government made citizenship education compulsory for every student in English schools. But as citizenship was taught through the existing curriculum, that is, through incorporating new topics into existing subjects, there were large variations in practice. The need for more comprehensive provision was addressed in a 2007 Curriculum Review led by Sir Keith Ajegbo. His final report set out a 'vision' that all schools should be 'actively engaged in nurturing in pupils the skills to participate in an active and inclusive democracy, appreciating and understanding difference.'[17] Despite the focus on 'diversity', the report spoke of a need to 'provide young people with a common sense of identity and belonging'.

The connection between citizenship education, diversity, and community cohesion became formalised in the new National Curriculum introduced into schools in 2008. Citizenship classes aimed to enable all young people to become 'responsible citizens who make a positive contribution to society'. In addition, a new theme, 'Identities and Diversity: living together in the UK' involved 'appreciating that identities are complex', 'considering the connections between the UK, Europe and the rest of the world' and 'exploring the diverse national, regional, ethnic and religious cultures, groups and communities in the UK and the connections between them.'[18] Citizenship classes effectively became a catch-all solution to a variety of social and political problems.

In 2013, following a change of government in the UK, the citizenship curriculum was again re-drafted.[19] Its new aim was to 'foster pupils' keen awareness and understanding of democracy, government and how laws are made and upheld.' It had a more national focus but remained an ill-defined subject that encompasses topics from personal financial planning to 'how laws are shaped and enforced'. Such broad content, combined with a focus on practical, local activities, left classes open to the different political enthusiasms of individual schools and teachers.

Post-Brexit, a number of headteachers and representatives of professional associations signed an open letter to then Education Secretary Justine Greening calling for a renewed commitment to the teaching of PSHE, Citizenship and Religion.[20] Their focus was not national, but global citizenship, whereby children are taught to think of themselves not as members of a nation, but of the world. In other words, the role of citizenship education, in substituting an international focus for affinity with the nation state, was to pose a direct challenge to the sentiments that were assumed to have led to British citizens voting to leave the EU. In this way, citizenship classes were also to distance children from the values of their parents, an older generation held responsible for the result of the 2016 referendum.

Citizenship classes encompass a political agenda that is hidden behind a rhetoric of 'values'. Children are encouraged to take on board a particular moral outlook without the capacity to disagree. This is reinforced through more traditional academic subjects such as geography. Three key themes of the geography curriculum are sustainability, globalisation and equality.[21] Sustainability speaks to one approach to addressing environmental concerns that is often anti-growth and anti-development. Yet rather than asking children to debate the benefits of fair trade versus free trade, or nuclear power versus renewables, they are expected to demonstrate the importance of sustainable development to local communities, particularly in the global south. Through such processes, the interests of a small group of curriculum planners are recast as universal moral values.

The history curriculum has likewise become a vessel for promoting political views, often presented as 'skills', in a way that seeks to steer children's attitudes away from those of their parents and community. For over five decades efforts have been underway to shift the focus of the history curriculum from a chronological national story to an emphasis on the present. In 1972, the Schools History Project 'launched a radically new content offer' which 'included topics strongly linked to present-day crises' such as Northern Ireland and the Arab–Israeli conflict, as well as 'world themes across time such as energy and medicine, and an emphasis on local history through the archaeology of the built and natural environment.'[22] This was, at least in part, a reaction to shifts in the academy that centered, 'black history, women's history and attention to indigenous peoples that sought to transcend and critique colonial lenses.'[23] This identitarian approach leaves history open to critical race theory-inspired movements to decolonise the curriculum.[24]

In 2010, the then Conservative government attempted to overhaul a history curriculum that had come to be seen as not just political but anti-British. Then Education Secretary Michael Gove pledged that 'all pupils will learn our island story' and went so far as to argue that 'this trashing of our past has to stop.' His announcement was criticised by teachers, academics, teaching unions, historians and the presidents of learned societies such as the Historical Association.[25]

In 2021, research by the Universities of Oxford and Reading found that 87 per cent of UK secondary schools had made substantial changes to history teaching – not to emphasise a national story but to address issues of diversity.[26] According to this study, the reasons cited included: 'a sense of social justice, to better represent the nature of history and the stimulus of recent events.' Seventy-two per cent of teachers claimed their classes covered the history of migration while 80 per cent said they engaged pupils in a study of Black and Asian British history. Most common was a focus on the post-war period, including the experiences of the 'Windrush generation' but many also reported teaching the black Tudors. Meanwhile, the UK's biggest teaching union published a report urging the decolonisation of 'every subject and every stage of the school curriculum.' It argues that every aspect of school life from the design of school classrooms to the structure of their daily routines have colonial roots.[27]

Subjects such as history and geography are used by schools and teachers to promote a distinct set of values that may be at odds with the values held by a pupil's parents. Not only is this not considered a problem, it is perceived by some educationalists as an opportunity to bring about social change. On matters such as climate change or gender identity, children are expected to educate their parents and other adults, rather than the other way round.

At one primary school in Birmingham, for example,

children are co-opted into policing their classrooms and playgrounds. If a teacher mis-speaks, pupils hold up brightly coloured posters highlighting the particular speech crime that has been committed. They are praised for shaming the teacher, compelling an apology and alerting fellow pupils to the incident. Each week, the two children who pursue this task most enthusiastically are rewarded with a certificate.[28] St Paul's Girls' School in London replaced the title 'head girl' with the more gender-neutral title 'head of school'. This sends a message to pupils and parents alike that the word 'girl' is outdated and offensive.[29]

Politicised schooling moves education away from the transmission of traditional bodies of knowledge that connect childen to their intellectual birthright. Instead of education enabling a conversation between the generations, politicised schooling breaks with the legacy of the past. In place of the knowledge that weaves a thread between children and their parents, grandparents, community and nation, pupils are expected to imbibe political values that are often in stark contrast to the values of an older generation.

Teachers as substitute parents

Alongside instructing pupils in beliefs and values that may run counter to the views of their parents, teachers encroach upon what was once assumed to be the responsibility of the family in relation to the health and wellbeing of their children. Increasingly, childhood is considered to be a state of vulnerability. As Abigail Shrier explores in her book *Bad Therapy*, children are now perceived to be at risk, both physically and mentally, from life experiences such as walking to school alone or falling out with friends, that would have been considered routine parts of growing up a generation or more ago.

A 2021 British Children's Play Survey found that children today have two years less freedom than their parents did at the same age. In practical terms, this means that most children today are 11 years old before they are allowed to play outside their home unsupervised compared to their parents who were nine when they achieved the same milestone.[30] In response, parents stand accused of being 'overprotective' and 'mollycoddling' their children.[31] But some rites of passage such as walking home from school alone are actively discouraged by schools. Although independent travel is not illegal, many primary schools now have policies in place to prevent children leaving school alone or collecting younger siblings.

One typical 'walking home alone policy' from a primary school in Yorkshire states:

> 'We believe that pupils in years 3, 4 and 5 should be still brought to and collected from school and this is our school policy. Therefore, as regards pupils in Year 6, we believe that you as parents need to decide whether your child is ready for the responsibility of walking to and from school alone.'[32]

The school assumes responsibility for children below the age of ten and makes a clear decision that they should not be allowed to walk home unaccompanied by a parent or other approved-adult. For children above the age of 10, this responsibility lies with parents. However, the school does not simply leave parents to decide for themselves what is in their child's best interests. It offers the following advice:

> 'In deciding whether your child is ready to walk to school you should assess any risks associated with the route and your child's confidence. Work with your children to build up their independence while walking to school through route finding, road safety skills and general awareness.'[33]

By telling parents both that younger children should not walk home unaccompanied and issuing guidance as to how such a decision for older children should be reached, the school positions itself, and not parents, as the experts in childhood. In other words, the act of telling parents that they should decide how their children get to and from school presumes that parents require advice and are subservient to the authority of teachers. When schools present walking home alone not as a taken-for-granted part of growing up but a process that requires expert advice and careful management, it is hardly surprising that many parents conclude it is better to take children to school by car. In 2022, 40 per cent of children aged 5-10 and 26 per cent of children aged 11-15 traveled to school by car.[34] But parents are warned that even this is not a risk-free option:

'Children who are driven to school do not have the opportunity to develop road awareness and are therefore more vulnerable when they start to walk to school independently.'[35]

A similar dynamic takes place around food. The Department for Education provides detailed guidance on school food standards which was last updated in February 2023.[36] This primarily relates to lunches provided by schools to children. In addition, the Department for Education offers guidance on 'creating a culture and ethos of healthy eating'.[37] This is reinforced by Ofsted which assesses the extent to which schools support children to 'make informed choices about healthy eating.'[38] As part of this inspection framework, schools are expected to demonstrate a 'whole school' approach to healthy eating. This means that school leaders are not just accountable for the lunches provided to children in the middle of the day, usually via a school canteen, but also for the lunches some children may bring from home, as a packed lunch. This means that although there is no official government guidance on packed lunches, and the Department for Education allows individual schools to decide what their policy is on food brought in from home, many schools do produce strict rules in order to comply with government guidance and Ofsted's inspection criteria. Individual schools are supported in this regard by local education authorities or multi-academy trusts. For example, Brighton and Hove City Council's Public Health Schools Programme provides 'packed lunch policy guidance' that provides a template policy document for schools to tailor to their own specific circumstances.[39]

As a result many schools, especially primary schools, now have 'packed lunch policies' that set out which foods are permissible. In terms of individual schools, one primary school in London can be taken as an example of typical policies. It instructs parents that lunch boxes should contain 'at least one portion of fruit and one portion of vegetables every day' and 'dairy food such as milk, cheese, yoghurt, fromage frais or custard everyday'. Chocolate, sweets and crisps are all prohibited.[40] Parents at another primary school in Bradford are informed that 'Staff on duty, midday supervisors and catering staff will monitor the contents of packed lunches' with 'serious concerns' highlighted to the school's Senior Management Team.[41]

School travel and lunch policies considerably expand the remit of teachers away from education and into all aspects of child-rearing. In the process, they undermine parents' confidence in making decisions about their own children's independence and safety. Parents are expected to defer to the advice of other adults who purport to be experts in their children. Under the newly elected Labour government, teachers may take on even more responsibility for child-rearing, including providing lessons in tooth brushing.[42]

Perhaps the most notable way in which schools assume expertise in and responsibility for areas other than education is in relation to child mental health. The Department for Education expects all schools to have a 'whole school' approach to promoting and supporting mental health and wellbeing. Among its 'eight key principles' are 'curriculum teaching and learning to promote resilience and support social and emotional learning', 'identifying the need for and monitoring the impact of interventions', 'targeted support and appropriate referral' and 'working with parents and carers'.[43] As with walking to school, we see acknowledgement of the role of parents but only from a starting assumption that child mental health falls under the remit of teachers, whether that is through the curriculum or by offering targeted support to individual pupils identified as struggling, or working with families by suggesting ways for parents to support their children.

Commonly used school mental health interventions include mindfulness,[44] meditation[45] and yoga.[46] Such activities might take place as part of Relationships, Sex and Health Education classes but government guidance suggests that teaching and learning should also take place with a view to focusing on a child's emotional responses in order to help them manage their 'thoughts, feelings and behaviour'.[47] One primary school in Greater Manchester outlines the kinds of activities it employs to meet these goals:

> 'Support is embedded in all classrooms and is part of the whole school approach. This is achieved through a variety of initiatives such as emotional registers, circle time, Relax Kids, daily mile, worry boxes in class and "My Happy Mind."'[48]

Activities such as 'emotional registers' act as 'temperature checks' asking children to observe and report on their feelings at various points throughout the school day. 'Circle time' can involve children in more open-ended discussion about their emotions with the teacher taking on the role of group therapist.

Clearly, teachers have a duty of care to seek help for children who are experiencing mental health problems. But the routine use of whole school interventions suggests that every child is considered to be in need of support and that it is the responsibility of schools, alongside or instead of parents, to care for a child's mental health. When children are expected to discuss their emotions in the context of the classroom, it is often their home lives, and the intimate details of their relationships with their parents they expose to public scrutiny. As we will explore in the next section, this sits within a broader cultural context that frequently identifies parents as a risk to their child's mental health. Indeed, one dominant assumption is that far from families providing a source of comfort to children, they may be the source of emotional problems. In this way, teachers as experts in child development at best assume responsibility for children's mental wellbeing in lieu of parents and, at worst, actively undermine family relationships.

Parents abdicating responsibility

In parallel with the expansion of the teacher's role emerges frustration that parents are failing to take responsibility for raising their children. 'British parents have forgotten their most basic responsibilities,'[49] bemoans one commentator, while an educationalist complains that 'teachers shouldn't have to do the parents' job, too.'[50] Those sympathetic towards parents argue that financial hardship, long working hours and social breakdown make family life more challenging today. A less charitable interpretation is that feckless, lazy or ignorant parents prefer screen time (for themselves or their offspring) in preference to the hard work of child rearing. Regardless of the explanation (or the accuracy of the sentiment) four main concerns recur: children do not know how to behave appropriately in a classroom; parents do not support regular attendance and children start school without being toilet trained or possessing the skills and knowledge required to begin formal education.

Behaviour

Teachers report that pupils behave badly in the classroom. Research conducted for the NASUWT teaching union found that more than one in ten teachers had been physically assaulted by a pupil in the past year with almost 20 per cent subjected to threats of physical assault and 60 per cent receiving verbal abuse from pupils. 'Back chat/rudeness' was reported by almost all survey respondents (97 per cent).[51] Research for the think tank Policy Exchange, conducted in 2018, found that 75 per cent of teachers reported low-level disruption occurring 'frequently' or 'very frequently' in their schools. Many knew of colleagues who had 'left the teaching profession because of bad behaviour'.[52] There is a consensus that pupil behaviour has deteriorated further since schools re-opened following Covid lockdowns. Research conducted in 2024 for the BBC found that 'A greater proportion of primary and secondary teachers reported pupils fighting, pushing and shoving compared with two years ago.'[53]

The BBC's research also suggests that one in five teachers has experienced online abuse from a parent or guardian, and a similar number has experienced verbal abuse. Teachers are concerned that such actions undermine their authority in the eyes of pupils and lead children to think that such behaviour is acceptable. 'It's no wonder children are so badly behaved. Just look at their parents,' writes one commentator.[54] Surprisingly, a similar conclusion is reached by researchers from the 'Mentally Healthy Schools' initiative, run by the Anna Freud centre, who note that 'behavioural problems and anger' may be a sign that children are being 'exposed to stresses' within the home environment. 'Children and young people may, for example, experience neglect, abuse, violence, poverty, witness domestic abuse, see parents or siblings go in and out of prison, among other things,' all of which can, according to the centre, manifest in a child's behaviour.[55]

Also of concern is a growing trend for parents to protest outside school gates. Parents in Birmingham demonstrated against a school's sex and relationships curriculum while parents in Batley protested against a teacher showing pupils a cartoon representation of the Prophet Muhammed, resulting in the teacher being forced into hiding.[56] Barclay Primary School in London faced closure after parents protested a ban on children wearing pro-Palestinian badges to school. Police became involved when the school received bomb threats. At a school in Cornwall, protests against 'harsh' school rules led to the police being called to disperse angry parents.[57]

When parents protest against lesson content or school rules they challenge the authority of teachers. They tell their children that, far from adults agreeing about the importance of discipline and good behaviour, parents do not support teachers in enforcing rules. Whether parents set a bad example to their children through their own behaviour, actively challenge teachers themselves, or inflict emotional harm on their children which leads to behavioural problems, the assumption is that parents cannot be relied upon to encourage their children to behave well in school.

Attendance

Regular attendance declined after schools reopened following Covid lockdowns. The rate of persistent absence (defined as missing at least 10 per cent of school sessions) rose from 13.1 per cent of all pupils in autumn 2019 to 24.2 per cent in autumn 2022.[58] This fell to 20.1 per cent in autumn 2023 – an improvement, but still far higher than pre-pandemic.[59] Explanations for the increase in absence include financial difficulties, mental health problems and unmet special educational needs. Research by the public opinion consultancy Public First points to a shift in parents' views on the importance of regular school attendance. Its report notes that some parents no longer believe it is their responsibility to ensure that their child is in school every day.[60] The number of parents taking children out of school for term-time holidays has also increased. Public First notes that term time holidays have become more socially acceptable across all socioeconomic groups. Polling for the think tank Centre for Social Justice suggests that 13 per cent of parents let children miss school for family holidays.[61]

Josephine Hussey, a primary school teacher from Cambridgeshire, comments on changing attitudes towards school attendance: 'school is no longer seen as compulsory … if a parent is struggling with getting their child to school for any reason, they're more likely to say, "just have a day off," than they were before.' She notes that the rise in parents working from home has contributed to this shift: 'in the past, if you had to go to the office, there was more reason to send your child into school.' The response to Covid-19 triggered a shift in attitude: 'Parents were trained to keep their child off sick at the first sign of a sniffle lest they be accused of contributing to the pandemic. Now, when a child is mildly unwell, parents are not quite sure what to do, and look to schools for guidance.' Ultimately, she argues, 'there's a sense of adults not insisting that their children attend.' Hussey puts this change down to a lack of confidence in parents. Whereas previously they may have trusted their own instincts and sent their children to school with minor ailments, now keeping children at home has become the more socially acceptable response.[62]

Toilet training

It is vital children can behave appropriately in a classroom in order to engage in learning and avoid disrupting the learning of others. For this reason, the ability to follow simple rules is considered a key part of children being 'school ready'. Teachers also expect children to be independent when it comes to personal tasks such as using the toilet, washing their hands, eating with a knife and fork, dressing after PE and doing up their coats and shoes. Although nurseries and pre-schools may play a role, it is largely assumed that parents will ensure their children can perform such tasks prior to starting school. While a majority of children can do such things, perhaps with minimal supervision in the first few weeks, there is concern over the number of children now starting school without this level of independence.

Teachers report that a growing number of children begin school without being fully toilet-trained. Some may still wear nappies while others may have frequent 'accidents'. This is time consuming for teachers and classroom assistants forced to take time out of the classroom to clean up after pupils or train them to use a toilet. Precise statistics on the proportion of children still in nappies are hard to find. One Multi-Academy Trust reports that out of a cohort of 450 pupils starting school, 30 were still in nappies.[63] A poll of 1,000 teachers suggests that 1 child in 4 is not toilet trained and teachers 'now spend a third of their day supporting pupils who are not school-ready.'[64] *The Guardian* reports that, 'school staff are on average diverting 2.5 hours a day away from teaching and towards supporting children who are not school-ready, which has a knock-on effect on pupils who lose around a third of learning time each day.'[65]

Delays in children's development have been blamed on Covid lockdowns. 'Pandemic babies are arriving at school still wearing nappies,' reads one headline.[66] Blame is also levelled at parents who prioritise working long hours and do not find the time to toilet train their toddlers, instead leaving the task to nursery staff.[67] Parents are similarly accused of spending time on their phones rather than toilet training their children. Other potential causes include the fact that children in the UK now start school at a younger age than in previous generations, with some starting formal education just days after their fourth birthday. In addition, as more children grow up in households where both parents are working full-time, higher numbers of children now attend nursery or other forms of pre-school childcare than a generation ago.[68] This may also prompt uncertainty as to whether responsibility for toilet training lies with parents or carers or leave young children confused when both parties adopt different methods of instruction.

At the same time, disposable nappies are both more sophisticated – children do not feel 'wet' after urinating and this may make toilet training more difficult – and also more convenient than cloth nappies, perhaps disincentivising early toilet training. Finally, there is far more awareness today about the potential psychological harms of getting toilet training 'wrong'. Parents are warned that both premature and delayed potty training may lead to children developing low self-esteem or insecurity.[69] When 'getting it wrong' is perceived as risking their child's mental health, parents may opt to leave the task to experts.

Teachers report other ways in which parents have not adequately prepared children for starting school. One survey suggests that more than a third (37%) of children cannot dress themselves while 29 per cent cannot eat or drink independently. This may mean time is taken away from teaching to help those struggling with such basic tasks. Of direct relevance to learning, the same survey suggests that almost half of pupils are unable to sit still, while 38 per cent struggle to play or share with others, and more than a quarter (28%) use books incorrectly, swiping or tapping as though they were using a tablet. It notes that more than a third of children start primary school unable to hold a pencil with a similar proportion unable to count to 10, while around a quarter of children are reported to lack basic language skills.[70]

At first glance, such reports seem shocking. However, we need to keep in mind that this refers to children potentially just days after their fourth birthday. Measuring a very young child's capacity to 'sit still' or 'share with others' is fraught with difficulty. Just as with some adults, these capacities often change with context. Perhaps what is most revealing about this survey is the different types of skills considered important for school-readiness. Many parents might, not unreasonably, assume that it is the job of the reception class teacher to teach children how to hold a pencil and count to ten. That such tasks are included alongside the ability to use a toilet or dress independently shines a light on the blurred boundaries between the perceived responsibilities of parents and teachers.

Conclusion

Discussions about the different roles of teachers and parents reveal considerable confusion over where the responsibilities of each party lie. Teachers blame parents for abdicating responsibility for raising their children while parents accuse teachers of overstepping the mark and interfering in their child's development. Above this confusion sits a growing sense that raising children requires specialist expertise and that the consequences of making mistakes can be catastrophic for a child's mental and emotional health. The danger, as we have shown, is that this confusion all too readily morphs into blame, with each party accusing the other of not fulfilling their obligations. This, in turn, can prompt conflict. When children see their parents and teachers disagreeing, collective adult authority is undermined. In the next section we explore the source of the confusion about roles and responsibilities.

2.

How did we get here?

Confusion about the specific responsibilities of parents and teachers, conflict between both parties and the undermining of adult authority more broadly are not new phenomena. For almost two centuries, experts in education, child development and parenting have questioned the potential for families to raise children in line with the latest psychological research. Policymakers have taken to heart arguments that the task of socialising the next generation is best left to those with specific qualifications and expertise. The impact of such decisions, played out over the course of many decades, has been to weaken the institution of the family and undermine the authority of parents. Yet, as we discuss below, this move to push responsibility for socialisation into schools has also fundamentally altered the nature of education and, in the process, severely damaged the authority of teachers who have been led to see themselves not as subject experts, able to transmit a body of knowledge to the next generation, but experts in a far more contested 'science' of child development. The result is that the authority of both teachers and parents is weakened. As such, disputes over roles and responsibilities occur frequently and are often played out in public.

Here, we explore two ways in which this process has taken place. First, we look at the impact of parenting experts upon family life and then we consider how schools became concerned with the socialisation of children rather than the transmission of knowledge.

What is socialisation?

Socialisation is the process by which children are taught to behave in ways that meet the expectations of society. The philosopher Michael Oakeshott defines it as 'an apprenticeship to adult life – teaching, training, instructing, imparting knowledge, learning etc. – governed by an extrinsic purpose.'[71] Socialisation, then, is the means by which children are made to conform to the norms and conventions of those around them. The process of socialisation involves teaching not as an end in itself, but for the extrinsic purpose of modifying children's behaviour.

At birth, babies are entirely dependent upon adults for their every need. As they grow, and very gradually gain independence, they learn not just how to meet their physical needs, but how to do so in ways that are deemed acceptable by those around them. For example, infants quickly learn to feed themselves. But in the process, and more slowly, they also learn social norms about what types of food to eat, when to eat and how to eat. Animals will eat when hungry or when food is available. Humans, in their first years of life, have to master not just the basic physical action of eating but also a sense that different foods are eaten at different times of the day, that food is often eaten at mealtimes, as a social ritual, and perhaps with crockery and cutlery. Although eating is a natural instinct, it is through socialisation that children learn acceptable ways in which to consume food.

Socialisation is rarely an explicit or formal process. Rather, it happens as children come to internalise the behaviours, attitudes and values of those around them. For this reason, the family, as the institution children are born into and the people children are closest to, plays a key role in relation to socialisation. Through immersion in the actions and expectations of parents and siblings, children pick up habits, attitudes and values while simultaneously learning behaviours such as how to communicate, how to use a toilet, how to eat, how to dress and how to interact with other people. As Oakeshott makes clear, 'The human family (whatever form it may take) is a practice devised, not for the procreation of children, nor merely for their protection, but for the early education of newcomers to the human scene.'[72] In other words, the socialisation of a new generation is the primary purpose of the family.

However, over the course of many decades, academics, policymakers and journalists have repeatedly questioned the capacity for the family to play this role. They have successfully established a narrative that presents leaving socialisation to the family as a threat to the life chances of individual children and a risk to society more broadly. In response, social workers, health professionals and cultural commentators have sought to present raising children not as an instinctive or natural part of family life but as a distinct task requiring the mastery of specific skills. Here, we explore the move from 'having children' to 'parenting' and how the growth of parenting experts undermines the role families have traditionally played in socialising the next generation.

The weakening of the family

The weakening of the institution of the family has been underway for almost two centuries. The French philosopher Jean Jacques Rousseau criticised parents as 'the agents who transmit false traditions and habits from one generation to the next'.[73] He argued that children had to be saved from authoritarian parents. In his sociological study of the family, *Haven in a Heartless World*, published in 1977, Christopher Lasch noted that, 'The family has been slowly coming apart for more than a hundred years.'[74]

The 'coming apart' of the family as an institution is reflected in statistics. Most recent figures show that the proportion of people aged 16 or older in England and Wales who are married or in a civil partnership is now below 50 per cent[75] – the lowest figure ever recorded. More children are born to mothers who are not married, than to two parents who are married.[76] In England and Wales, the birth rate has been declining since 2010 and was 1.49 children per woman in 2022, down from 1.55 in 2021.[77] It seems that significantly fewer people today aspire to marry and have children than in previous generations. This means that families, collectively, are less significant as an institution within broader society.

Beyond these statistics, the family has been 'coming apart' because its meaning has diminished. Families are no longer understood as an authoritative, private unit responsible for reproducing social life. Rather, families are understood as a set of fluid and provisional relationships premised upon contingent emotional bonds. The family still plays a social function in relation to raising the next generation but – as we explore below – rather than the authority of the parent being definitive, parents themselves are expected to defer to expert guidance. As a result, the family is weaker today than ever before, both in numerical terms and in what the family represents.

With family life having been subjected to external, expert scrutiny and made the subject of repeated panics for almost two centuries, what is perhaps remarkable is not the collapse of the family, but that it endures. That such a significant proportion of adults do still choose to marry and have children suggests that people in general have not simply given up on family life. Rather, it is the pressure of influences outside of the family that have undermined the institution. The family, and its primary purpose of socialisation, has been subjected to decades of scrutiny, criticism and expert intrusion. As sociologist Frank Furedi notes, 'The willingness of experts to by-pass parents and socialize children directly has been evident for well over a century.'[78]

From being a mum to doing parenting

As early as the nineteenth century, self-declared experts were beginning to challenge the idea that parents had an instinctive sense of how best to care for their children. There was concern that, left to their own devices, fathers would be ruthless disciplinarians while mothers would be over-indulgent. A new breed of campaigners sought 'to educate and influence the mother and make her 'instinct' secondary to their 'science''.[79] Experts assumed that moulding model citizens required 'the displacement of folk knowledge by scientific insight.'[80] In the first decades of the twentieth century, the authority of science increasingly overshadowed the insights and values of ordinary people. Traditional family routines were considered to be old fashioned, outdated and inefficient. There was a move to limit the role of parents and 'to assign the wider task of child socialization to the helping professions.'[81]

The newly-established discipline of sociology focused upon the family. Sociologists documented the ways in which the traditional family was considered unfit to meet the new challenges facing a rapidly industrialising world. As Brigitte Berger notes in her book *The Family in the Modern Age*, intellectuals argued that there were moral and financial reasons why the state had to compensate for the shortcomings of the family. In response, child guidance clinics and family support programs were enacted and the numbers of trained 'family experts' proliferated. The aim was to change individual behaviour deemed to be problematic 'by getting involved in the inner workings of the family.'[82]

Since this time, expert guidance to parents has changed so often that 'rules' often seem to come full circle. In one generation, new mothers are advised to implement strict routines, the next they are told to be flexible and led by their baby's needs. Years later, routines are back in vogue. One thing that remains constant is the presence of experts. They simply reinvent themselves and declare new 'evidence' demands new guidance. Berger describes 'the quasi-official conviction that anyone who had the proper qualifications (acquired by means of credentials) was able to carry out the demanding tasks associated with the care and socialization of children, perhaps even better than parents themselves could.'[83]

As we explore below, one impact of the emergence of the new science of child rearing was to move more responsibility for a child's social, moral and physical development away from the family altogether and locate it within the school. In the 1960s, the growing demand that teachers fulfil goals of socialisation was questioned. The influential Plowden Report into the future of primary education, published in 1967, notes that 'some teachers are anxious about the extent to which the school is taking the responsibility for the child's welfare and thus undermining the responsibility, as some would put it, of parents.'[84] It is unimaginable that such a statement could be written today because, for the past five decades, there has been a marked escalation of the narrative that parents are unable to raise children without external, expert intervention.

Prior to the 1970s, bringing up children was less a distinct practice performed by specific individuals but an everyday part of community and family life. Parenting emerged as families became smaller and home life more privatised. As Ellie Lee *et al.* explore in their book *Parenting Culture Studies*, the shift from *being* a parent to *doing* parenting was, from the outset, 'associated with the view that parent–child relationships are problematic or deficient'.[85] Parents were not expected to trust their own instincts but to defer to experts. This transformed family life from something that happened instinctively and spontaneously to something that happened consciously and deliberately. Adults no longer became parents but were expected to engage in parenting – a distinct practice requiring a particular set of skills which was best 'conducted under the watchful gaze of experts'. One impact of this process was that parents simultaneously had their authority undermined while being held responsible for much more. Discipline, for example, was no longer seen as a collective task involving every adult in a community, but the specific responsibility of parents alone.

Parenting without authority

The 'professionalisation' of parenting escalated rapidly from the mid-1990s. New Labour's Sure Start programme provided not just badly-needed nursery provision but parenting classes too. The assumption that not just 'problem' parents, but all parents, would benefit from official guidance became entrenched. As Furedi noted at the time, 'Current social policy is oriented towards altering the behaviour of parents, in an approach that has been described as 'New Labour's resocialization programme.''[86] The result of such interventions has been to consign parents to the role of 'assistant manager' in relation to their children. The family is no longer a moral unit but simply a mechanism for enacting formal guidance.

This process took its crudest form in Scotland where

the Scottish National Party tried to implement legislation allotting each child a 'named person' who would act as an intermediary between parent and state, to advocate for the child and safeguard his or her welfare. In practice, the only time a child needs an external advocate is when their wishes contradict those of their parents. In this way, the very existence of a 'named person' – a 'kindly intruder' into family life – undermines the authority of parents. The SNP ultimately failed to pass its named person legislation into law, but the message that parents cannot be trusted to act in the best interests of their own children and experts from outside the family have an important role to play in raising children was widely accepted.[87]

Over the course of the past two decades, parenting experts have become household names and their 'theories', formalised into parenting classes, have been promoted by policymakers as the solution to everything from childhood obesity to poor academic attainment.[88] At the same time, the targeting of expertise has shifted from 'problem' families to all mothers and fathers. Lee points to the 'increasingly consensual assumption that all parents benefit from parent training and parenting support.' The dominant message communicated to mothers and fathers is that the health, welfare, and success (or lack of it) of their children can be directly attributed to the decisions they make about matters like feeding their children; 'parenting', parents are told, is both the hardest and most important job in the world.[89] As Lee *et al.* argue, 'It is this more recent turn towards an explicit focus on the parent and their behaviour that emerges as the general, distinctive attribute of the contemporary term 'parenting' and the determinism it brings with it.'[90] In other words, parents are told that, at the very same time, they are entirely responsible for every aspect of their child's development and that they do not know enough to carry out this role adequately. This, understandably, prompts a great deal of confusion and anxiety in parents.

The upshot, as *Parenting Culture Studies* explores, is a far more 'intensive' approach to raising children, involving vast amounts of time, energy, and money, as well as deference to carefully selected self-styled gurus. As Lee et al. point out, this intensive parenting is 'certainly not followed in practice by every mother' but the prevalence of expert guidance comes to be 'implicitly or explicitly, understood as the proper approach to the raising of a child by the majority of mothers'.[91] This means that even though parents frequently 'break the rules', for example, by switching from breast to formula feeding, using technology to pacify toddlers or ignoring bed times, they do so self-consciously. An awareness of an expert-approved approach to raising children is now pervasive.

The rise of parenting expertise has undermined the authority of parents. The prevalence of official instruction makes parents' instinctive ways of behaving in relation to their children seem second best. In addition, in order to justify their own position, experts must constantly seek out new problems and risks associated with leaving child rearing to parents. Experts, as Furedi makes clear, 'know that if they are to assume authority for the socialization of the child, they need constantly to question the authority of the parent.'[92] When children themselves become aware of approved parenting practices, they come to see where their own parents fall short.

Ultimately, parenting can never work successfully as an expert-led practice because it is seeking to solve a problem – the collapse of parental authority – that experts themselves caused. Today's parents end up being placed in an impossible position: they are tasked with raising children while robbed of all authority and reminded constantly of the harm that can be inflicted if they get things wrong.

Parents as a source of psychological harm

The notion that parents pose a particular threat to their children's mental health is not new. As poet Philip Larkin wrote in 1971:

> They f**k you up, your mum and dad.
> They may not mean to, but they do.
> They fill you with the faults they had
> And add some extra, just for you.[93]

While this may have been shocking five decades ago, today it is accepted as common sense. Nowadays, an entire industry of counsellors, self-help books and therapeutic practices is focused upon 'healing' adults of the trauma inflicted during childhood by their parents.

What drives this view is a belief in 'parental determinism': the notion that every characteristic and attribute of a person – from academic success to obesity and from wealth to happiness – can be traced back to their childhood and their relationship with their parents. As Berger noted more than two decades ago, 'all individual deviations from idealized behavioural norms tended to be reduced to psychological malfunctions that were held to have their origin in defective family interaction.'[94] Lee *et al.* make a similar point today: 'Parental action and behaviour, in everyday, ordinary life, is considered to have a determining, causal impact on a child's future happiness, healthiness, and success; in the twenty-first century, 'parental determinism' is very strong.'[95]

In this way, schools and health professionals are expected to remove children from psychologically harmful relationships or, more often, provide them with a therapeutic environment to lessen the harm caused by the home and protect them from further harm. The upshot, as Furedi argues, is that even if parents are not causing their children emotional harm, 'the belief that parents lack the competence to nurture the emotional development of their children is far more widespread today than in the past.'[96] Underlying every interaction between parent and child is a fear of the psychological harm that could be caused by making mistakes. As Berger notes, 'The "parenting deficit" is blamed for children's mental health problems, educational difficulties, anti-social behaviour, and poor coping skills, and the destructive consequences of bad parenting last throughout a person's life.'[97] Parental ability has been cast into doubt in a culture sociologist Ashley Frawley describes as shaped by 'belief in the vulnerability of children, but also of adults.'[98] Parents are a source of damage to their children but they are also victims themselves, with their own psychological problems, just as in need of professional help as their children.

Abolish the family

Fear of the damage that can be caused by poor parenting combines with a more political sense that the family is a threat to broader social progress. By rooting children in past traditions and old values, families are blamed for hindering the take-up of more progressive thinking particularly around gender identity and LGBTQ+ rights. This sentiment began to take hold in the 1960s when, as Berger describes, 'the counterculture's vision of a life free of boundaries and restrictions made it virtually inevitable that the lifestyle and values [of the traditional, nuclear family] came to be seen as the major obstacle standing in the way of its realization.'[99]

The demands of motherhood meant family life, and

children in particular, came to be seen as holding back women's freedom by second wave feminists such as Betty Friedan. The family was no longer perceived by a cultural elite to be a 'haven in a heartless world' but the site of women's oppression at the hands of the patriarchy. It was assumed that women's liberation meant liberation from the family. Today, such arguments are carried to their radical, logical conclusion by activists like Sophie Lewis. In her book *Abolish the Family*, Lewis presents a relentlessly grim depiction of the nuclear family. She argues: 'the family is where most of the rape happens on this earth, and most of the murder. No one is likelier to rob, bully, blackmail, manipulate, or hit you, or inflict unwanted touch, than the family.'[100] The family is, she concludes, 'a shitty contract pretending to be biological necessity.'[101] In order for people to live freely, and as their true selves, the nuclear family must be abolished, Lewis contends.

Although Lewis's views are extreme and provocatively expressed, the sentiment she taps into, that the nuclear family is a risk to social progress, individual free expression and everyone's mental health, is not unusual. As Ashley Frawley notes in relation to the European Union's policies on the family, so-called 'rainbow families' of migrants or comprising people with diverse gender identities or sexualities are celebrated but the word 'mother' is rarely used.[102] Berger argues that 'The anti-conventional family agenda has entered the public arena with considerable fanfare. In some school districts in the United States this agenda has been adopted lock, stock and barrel.'[103]

Conclusion

Over the course of many decades parents have been encouraged to defer continually to the authority of experts.

They have been told that they are responsible for their child's future well-being and that failure to follow expert guidance may inflict irreparable psychological harm upon their child. Parents now face a bind. They are expected to parent authoritatively while having had to give up the source of their authority in the home – the instinctive knowledge and insight they have in relation to their own children and family circumstances. Having raised concern about the adequacy of parents, professionals such as teachers, counsellors, social workers and parenting experts assume a far larger role in relation to socialising children, but they do so while blaming parents for abdicating responsibility.

In practice, this undermining of parental authority and – significantly – confidence, means that teaching children about sex and relationships, for example, becomes far more fraught with difficulty than it may have been in the past when children were expected to pick up such knowledge informally from conversations with peers and extended family members. Today, parents know that teachers will cover such topics as part of the school curriculum. What's more, they assume that teachers, unlike parents, are familiar with the latest thinking and correct terminology. On top of all this, they know that the consequence of teaching the 'wrong' ideas may leave their child vulnerable. It becomes safest and easiest to leave sex and relationships education to schools. Yet, when they do so, they weaken their own position in the eyes of their child and diminish the status of the family in society more broadly. As a final blow, despite having done what is expected of them, parents find themselves accused of being lazy or feckless for abdicating their responsibilities.

The same can be said for toilet training. What was once a routine part of raising children has become problematised. Experts tell parents that there are correct ways to approach the task and that failure to follow approved methods might result in psychological harm to the child. At the same time, there is growing awareness that teachers will step in and fulfil this role if parents do not. For some parents, leaving the task of toilet training to teachers comes to make sense. The danger now is that this same process occurs in relation to brushing children's teeth. As we explore below, this is clearly a problem, although not necessarily one of parents' own making.

3.

A crisis point? From education to socialisation

As we have noted, Oakeshott was clear about the purpose of the family being 'the early education of newcomers to the human scene.'[104] As parents have only partial knowledge of the 'human scene', education has also, historically, played a key role in relation to socialisation. As the American philosopher and psychologist John Dewey notes: 'Beings who are born not only unaware of, but quite indifferent to, the aims and habits of the social group have to be rendered cognizant of them and actively interested. Education, and education alone, spans the gap.'[105] Just as with the family, this is rarely an explicit process.

If we consider education to be primarily concerned with the transmission of knowledge from one generation to the next, then, through the selection of knowledge worthy of passing on, and the process of inculcating children into their intellectual birthright, education comes to be understood as the formal means by which a new generation is introduced to an already existing world. Literature, history, and even mathematics convey assumptions about what it means to be human and a member of society at a particular point in time. In this way, the intergenerational transmission of knowledge reveals to children the nature of the society of which they are a part. The transmission of knowledge is inherently an act of socialisation.

The relationship between education and socialisation is further linked because the transmission of knowledge occurs as a formal process that, for the most part, takes place in schools. In going to school, children are separated from their families, brought out of the home environment and made to enter the public realm. School attendance forces children to confront the world and see themselves in relation to their peers. Dewey notes that:

> 'The development within the young of the attitudes and dispositions necessary to the continuous and progressive life of a society cannot take place by direct conveyance of beliefs, emotions, and knowledge. It takes place through the intermediary of the environment.'[106]

Schools, as institutions, play an important role in this process of socialising a new generation.

Children learn about the society they have been born into through the transmission of knowledge, but attitudes, values and behavioural norms are also shaped through the interactions that take place in the school. The authority of the teacher, and his or her capacity to inspire children and enforce expected standards of behaviour is central to the school's role in relation to socialisation. But by bringing children together into a community, schools also play an informal socialising role. Dewey writes that, 'The intermingling in the school of youth of different races, differing religions, and unlike customs creates for all a new and broader environment.'[107] Similarly, the philosopher Hannah Arendt described schools as 'the institution that we interpose between the private domain of home and the world in order to make the transition to the world possible'; meaning that, to a child, 'school represents the world, although it is not yet actually the world'.[108]

Socialisation, then, is an ever-present but implicit process occurring at home, school and within communities.

Crucially, it does not draw attention to itself. As Dewey makes clear, effective socialisation takes place through the medium of the environment, not through direct instruction. Schools instil values in children not through timetabled classes or even talks given in assembly. Instead, values are enacted through the school environment. Pupils are not given lessons on the need to respect adults; instead, they are taught to call teachers 'sir' or 'miss' and to be quiet when teachers are talking, and are disciplined for rudeness towards members of staff. Similarly, in the past, children were not given lectures on the importance of competitiveness to ambition and self-improvement. Instead, schools held sports days, awards ceremonies and encouraged rivalry between different forms.

One value in particular shaped what happened in schools: respect for knowledge. Knowledge was presented to children as an end in itself: they were expected to leave school knowing more than they did when they began. Shared curricular knowledge bonded children to one another, to previous generations and to the shared historical memory of their community and nation. The discipline and rituals enacted by teachers within the institution of the school were not without purpose: they were designed to create an environment that supported children's submission to the intellectual authority of the teacher. Teachers, in transmitting knowledge, were also shaping mental habits. For this reason, discipline refers to academic subjects as well as behaviour.

Schools have, at different times, sought to instil in children particular attitudes and values such as obedience, religious piety, national pride, or respect for multiculturalism and sexual equality. Such values rarely attracted the ire of parents because they were shared by most adults in society. Schools reflected the broader culture: they were not attempting to change it. Just as there was general agreement about the values to instil in children, so too was there a general consensus about what schools should teach. Beyond the 'three R's' there was an expectation that children would master the literary canon, key periods in national history, scientific principles and geographical features. Preserving and passing on canonical knowledge made schools inherently conservative institutions. Rather than seeking to change society in their own image, teachers looked to the past to determine what would be of value for the future. The ethos of many schools, represented in rules, uniforms and rituals, was rooted in tradition.

Crucially, although education and socialisation are intrinsically connected, and come together in the location of the school and the role of the teacher, they have quite distinct goals. Education aims at the transmission of knowledge as an end in itself. Children are introduced to their intellectual birthright but what they do with this knowledge in the future is for them alone to determine. Socialisation, on the other hand, aims to instil pre-determined attitudes and behaviours, and as Oakeshott notes, it is 'governed by an extrinsic purpose'. The aim of socialisation is the inculcation within individuals of the norms, values and behaviours necessary for participation in society.

Values, and even ways of behaving, can be inculcated as a consequence or a by-product of learning having taken place, but real intellectual growth, or mastery of knowledge, cannot occur as a result of socialisation alone. Bending the transmission of knowledge to the primary purpose of socialisation prevents it being of intrinsic value. For this reason, when socialisation becomes the primary goal of schooling, schools can no longer truly be described as educational institutions, if education is properly understood as the transmission of knowledge. Nonetheless, this move away from education and towards socialisation as the purpose of the school has been underway for a long time.

As we have already noted, a key driver pushing schools to play a more pro-active role in relation to socialisation has been persistent scepticism about the capacity of parents to fulfil such responsibilities adequately. Such sentiments were evident in the first calls to make schooling compulsory. The philosopher John Stuart Mill argued that state education could free children from the 'uncultivated' influence of their parents while French sociologist Emile Durkheim considered the very purpose of education was to 'adapt the child to the social environment in which he is destined to live.'[109] In practice, schools and families reached at times uneasy compromises over who held responsibility for a child's moral, spiritual, intellectual and behavioural development. However, as Furedi notes, over the course of the past century, responsibility has 'gradually shifted from the parent to the school.'[110]

Shift to child-centred education

Classical education is centred upon knowledge: the key questions facing educators are what knowledge is worthy of transmission and how best it can be imparted. Progressive education, on the other hand, is centred upon socialisation. The key questions facing progressive educators are which values should be inculcated and how best to promote child development. Classical education considers teachers to be subject experts with knowledge the source of their authority in the classroom. Progressive education, on the other hand, considers teachers to be experts in pedagogy with their authority coming from their knowledge of child development.

Dewey made the case for child-centred education in his 1916 book *Democracy and Education*. His work met with a receptive audience: dominant views about education and the nature of childhood were already being questioned. As the educationalist E.D. Hirsch notes, attitudes towards childhood that first emerged in the Romantic period were becoming increasingly fashionable by the end of the nineteenth century. He points to the influence in Dewey's work of Romantic poets such as Wordsworth and Coleridge who expressed an almost pantheistic sentiment that God was present in nature. For people to come close to God, what they needed was not formal education but opportunities for their mind to develop naturally in 'interchange with the natural world'.[111]

Similar sentiments had been expressed by the philosopher Jean-Jacques Rousseau in his masterpiece, *Emile*. Classical education assumes knowledge is rooted in truth, truth is rooted in God, and the role of the teacher is to reveal God's will to children through knowledge. In *Emile*, Rousseau shows that children have innate goodness and the role of the teacher is to keep children from knowledge of the world in order for their intrinsic goodness to be revealed. As Hirsch puts it, 'The classical aim of education was to correct nature through civilization. The romantic aim of education is to correct civilization through nature.'[112] He points out that by the 1840s, Horace Mann made reference to the 'development' of the mind seventeen times in his reports to the Massachusetts Board of Education.[113] Although Dewey has become most firmly associated with the progressive education movement, his argument, that overly rigid direction in the classroom risked squashing what was natural within the child, found fertile ground.

Within three decades of the publication of *Democracy*

and Education, ideas about the natural development of the child had become almost universally accepted in American schools and would soon make their way across the Atlantic. In the process, classical education was written off as unremittingly boring with traditional teachers accused of being authoritarian rather than authoritative. As Hirsch notes, education today is still dominated by the idea that education should follow the natural course of a child's individual development, meaning that nothing should be imposed upon the child before they are considered naturally ready. In practice, this means 'that hands-on simulations and projects are better than artificial, "merely verbal," "rote learning"; that the subjects studied are less important than developing critical thinking skills, since facts can always be looked up.'[114]

Perhaps ironically, promoting the natural development of the child did not mean trusting parents to know what was best for their offspring. Instead it meant that teachers needed to be trained in a new science of pedagogy. Teachers, not parents, were to be experts in childhood. For children's natural development to occur, children needed to be removed from the influence of the home environment and placed within schools, where teachers had attained the moral and intellectual resources necessary to socialise children correctly. This called into question the uneasy compromises that had been established between school and home and breached the trust between teachers and parents.

Today, teacher training incorporates elements of psychology and cognitive science. Child-centered principles remain but they are channelled into a psychological approach to learning, therapeutic concern with mental health and a behaviourist approach to discipline. As Furedi points out, 'A new group of experts claimed that their science entitled them to be the authoritative voices on issues that were hitherto perceived as strictly pertaining to the domain of personal and family life.'[115] Positioning teachers as experts in childhood undermines the status of parents. But it also, inadvertently, undermines the teacher's own authority too.

Shift to a future orientation

A focus on children rather than knowledge shifts education away from the legacy of the past and orients it towards the future. Rather than teachers passing on to children their intellectual inheritance, they seek to predict the skills and attributes that will be needed by society in the future. This point was made explicit by Dewey, who argued that, 'As a society becomes more enlightened, it realizes that it is responsible not to transmit and conserve the whole of its existing achievements, but only such as make for a better future society.'[116] Although he is right that the problem of selection lies at the heart of the school curriculum, selecting from 'existing achievements' allows teachers to apply the 'test of time'. It becomes possible to judge what is of enduring significance.

Orienting the school curriculum towards the future makes this impossible. Rather than considering what has stood the test of time, teachers are asked to predict what might be of relevance to a society that does not yet exist. Dewey makes this explicit: 'The scheme of a curriculum must take account of the adaptation of studies to the needs of the existing community life; it must select with the intention of improving the life we live in common so that the future shall be better than the past.'[117] Writing shortly after Dewey, another American educationalist, George S. Counts, went further. He argued that, 'If schools are to be really effective, they must become centers for the building, and not merely for the contemplation, of our civilisation.'[118] This hands tremendous power to teachers. They are no longer simply to transmit existing knowledge for children, as adults, to interpret and use as they see fit. Now, teachers are to determine for themselves the direction of a better future society and train children to meet such ends. As we consider below, this paves the way for politics to enter the classroom and with it, further division between school and home.

The crisis of socialisation

Turning education towards the science of child development and the creation of a better future society moves schools away from goals related to the transmission of knowledge. This has a devastating impact on education.

As Counts, writing in 1932 makes clear, when the socialisation of children becomes an end in itself, schools become a promised solution to a wide range of social problems:

> 'Faced with any difficult problem of life we set our minds at rest sooner or later by the appeal to the school. We are convinced that education is the one unfailing remedy for every ill to which man is subject, whether it be vice, crime, war, poverty, riches, injustice, racketeering, political corruption, race hatred, class conflict or just plain original sin.'[119]

Writing in 1954, Arendt notes a decline in school standards that occurred between the mid-nineteenth and mid-twentieth century, attributing it to a 'crisis of authority in education':

> '... pedagogy has developed into a science of teaching in general in such a way as to be wholly emancipated from the actual material taught. A teacher, so it was thought, is a man who can simply teach anything; his training is in teaching,

not in the mastery of any particular subject. […] An education without learning is empty and therefore degenerates with great ease into moral emotional rhetoric.'[120]

Almost a century later, we can see that the list of problems to which education is the apparent solution has changed, but the idea that the goal of the school is to resolve social issues is firmly entrenched. Today, government ministers and campaigners alike look to schools to tackle mental health problems, racism, homophobia, obesity, and climate change; and to inoculate children against the harms of pornography, social media bullying, misinformation and smoking. At times it can seem as if the answer to every problem is 'put it on the curriculum'. In the process, learning for its own sake is replaced by behaviour modification. Counts indicates what this means in practice: 'The school must shape attitudes, develop tastes, and even impose ideas.'[121] The upshot is that socialisation becomes the end point of schooling. Oakeshott makes clear the consequences of this approach: 'When to teach is identified with "socialization," education becomes the engagement to teach nothing.'[122]

The impact of this shift – from socialisation as a by-product of education focused on the transmission of knowledge to socialisation as the primary goal of schooling – cannot be underestimated. Oakeshott labels it 'the most momentous occurrence of this century'.[123] Even though children may still be taught subject knowledge, the socialisation imperative means that this is very different from the transmission of knowledge as an end in itself. As we noted in Chapter One, even academic subjects are now given political ends. Teaching literature, geography, and history has become intrinsically linked to the explicit promotion of contested views, rather than knowledge. Furthermore, these are the views of policy makers and pedagogues, and do not necessarily have broader purchase within society. This means they may be at odds with the values of a child's parents and trigger conflict between school and home. This poses a fatal challenge to the task of inducting a new generation into the norms of an existing society. Socialisation, to be effective, requires all adults to share in a common set of values in order to present them to children as universal expectations. When children come to realise that parents and teachers disagree, the project of socialisation collapses.

As we have noted, the assumption that schools have to correct the impoverished moral influence of the home undermines the authority of parents who must themselves defer to the presumed expertise of the teacher, not just in subject knowledge but in child development. But it also undermines the authority of teachers who are no longer a source of knowledge but learners themselves, just like their pupils. With no special knowledge to impart, teachers have little basis to command respect. Furedi notes that within education, 'a palpable loss of adult confidence has encouraged a growing reliance on expertise and motivational techniques.'[124] In other words, when the science of pedagogy determines the actions of the teacher, rather than her own moral judgement, no one assumes ultimate responsibility for either educating or socialising the next generation. The upshot is that children are not taught to treat parents or teachers with respect but with suspicion; they do not see adults as a source of wisdom and experience but as outdated and problematic.

Experts in morality

For some teachers, the collapse of their authority as subject experts, and the collapse of adult authority more broadly, together with the imperative to orient education towards the needs of a future society, leaves them with little sense of purpose in the classroom other than the promotion of their own political beliefs. It is not the case that teachers are so in thrall to political objectives that they no longer see teaching subject knowledge as important. Rather, it is because passing on subject knowledge is no longer seen as a worthwhile end in itself that the transmission of political values is able to lend a sense of purpose to teaching.

When teachers come to assume that the values they have to promote are superior to those of the home, parents are viewed not just as inadequate but in need of re-education. Pupils are encouraged to challenge the prejudices of their parents and to get them to adopt expert-approved views. This is a process Furedi has termed 'socialisation in reverse': a phenomenon where children are entrusted with the mission of socializing their elders.[125]

He explains it is a reversal in authority relations that has 'dramatic consequences for inter-generational interaction'.[126] This takes place in school as well as at home. An example of this process in action is relayed by the headteacher of a Birmingham primary school recounts the day, 'the children ran into my office one playtime and said, "Miss, Miss, something terrible has happened… one of the supervisors has just taken a skipping rope off a boy and said boys don't skip." They were rightly absolutely horrified. It was brilliant that they ran in to tell me.' As a result of the children's intervention, the playground supervisor had to attend a professional-conduct meeting and now no longer works at the school. Regardless of what one thinks of the appropriateness of the supervisor's comment, this is a clear illustration of this trend: children are praised for policing the behaviour of adults, rather than seeing adults as figures of authority.

Conclusion

Schools have been moving away from education and towards socialisation as their central purpose for almost two centuries. As a result, academic standards have fallen as teachers no longer carry weight as subject experts. For socialisation to occur explicitly, and not through the passing on of knowledge, new subjects such as citizenship and sexuality education have been introduced onto the curriculum. These new lessons represent an attempt to convey attitudes and behavioural norms directly. The perceived need for such lessons suggests elite educators lack confidence in both parents and subject knowledge to adequately convey appropriate values. Teachers undermine parents by taking on the task of socialisation. But the direct involvement of schools in socialisation has repercussions for teachers who need the support of parents in reinforcing behavioural expectations. At very least, this sows confusion about the demarcation of roles and responsibilities.

By teaching attitudes and values distinct from subject knowledge, the curriculum becomes increasingly politicised, further fuelling tensions between school and home. Rather than children coming to internalise the behaviours, attitudes and values of those around them, children learn that neither their parents nor their teachers have the authority to impose their will. They learn that there are few commonly held values and most behavioural expectations are negotiable. What results is not just an intellectual crisis but a crisis in socialisation. Once routine tasks such as toilet training and teaching children how to eat, how to behave in public and how to conduct themselves in relation to others are no longer carried out automatically and instinctively. They are problematised and contested.

4.

What should be done?

Today, teachers are encouraged to be 'child-centred' and, through the curriculum, guide pupils' social, political, moral and even sexual development. Schools care for children's mental wellbeing, instruct parents on appropriate lunch foods and issue guidance on when children are able to walk home alone. Parents, meanwhile, are encouraged not to trust their instincts but to follow advice from midwives, health visitors, social workers, teachers, counsellors and self-styled 'parenting experts' on how to bring up their children.

But when professionals accept a role in relation to child rearing there is no limit to the tasks that can be taken off parents and handed over to experts. The Labour Party's Child Health Action Plan proposes tooth brushing classes, more child mental health counsellors, breakfast clubs, a ban on flavoured-vapes and a national register of children not in school. The new Labour government may go further than ever before in taking responsibility for children's upbringing. 'I'm up for a fight over nanny state accusations,' declared Labour leader Keir Starmer, 'for a government to say "well that's none of our business," I just think is fundamentally wrong'.[127]

The consequence of this more overt 'nannying' is confusion about who is responsible for raising the next generation. Each new responsibility taken on by the school further changes the role of both teachers and parents. Parents are either wrong or are viewed as serving only a very limited purpose. Relationships between home and school become formalised through home school contracts or the language of 'partnerships'; this shift speaks to a recognition that informal relationships have broken down. Rather than genuine allies in the project of raising the next generation, parents and teachers are at best 'partners' and at worst competitors.

The child, in the context of the home school partnership, is the source of moral legitimacy for both teacher and parent. Reduced to 'managers of the child' parents and teachers are forced to compete for influence. In the process, children become aware that adult authority is fractured. Rather than collective solidarity between different groups of adults and collective responsbility for raising the next generation, there is blame and accusation. Discipline, as Lee *et al* note, is

> '...rarely discussed as a community task or the responsibility of adult society as a whole, whereby adults in general need to take on the demanding responsibility of working out what the role of discipline might be, as part of what it means to 'grow up'. Rather, discipline is discussed as a 'parenting strategy''.[128]

This makes discipline more limited in scope and less impactful across society as a whole.

When adult authority is weakened, socialising the next generation into existing norms and values becomes more challenging. Adults fear the consequences of imposing their will. Deference to experts risks no one assuming responsibility for raising children in the here and now. Few are able to put children under pressure to conform with the attitudes, values and ways of behaving that society deems acceptable. Evidence for a crisis of socialisation – an undermining of adult authority and an abdication of collective responsibility to the next generation – can be seen in conflicts between school and home; children being unsure how to behave, or behaving badly; a lack of respect for cultural traditions or older generations; and a lowering of expectations, for example, some children starting school unable to use a toilet.

Collective adult responsibility, such as it still exists, is now channelled through formal institutions such as nurseries, schools, social workers, health visitors and local council provision. This means that the crisis of socialisation accelerated over Covid lockdowns, when formal institutions either closed or operated remotely at the same time as children and parents were isolated from friends, relatives and neighbours. The social contract between the state and families suffered irreparable damage. Persistent absence from school continues to be a major problem.[129] Yet, as Lee *et al* note, although parents report having missed practical sources of support (schools, playgrounds, playgroups, medical appointments etc) 'almost no one reported missing parenting 'advice' or 'parenting support' programmes.'[130]

Both the transformation of schools into institutions more concerned with child development than the transmission of subject knowledge and the growing influence of parenting experts extend over many decades. Today, although most children are still raised in families and attend schools, these institutions have a very different meaning, and play a very different role, than they did in the past. Without any of the intrinsic authority once inherent in their role, teachers and parents are forced to compete as 'managers' of an appropriate 'childhood experience' rather than an apprenticeship for entry into society.

As this report has shown, the unravelling of adult authority and the crisis of socialisation have occurred slowly, over many decades. This means there are no 'quick fix' policy solutions to resolve today's problems. However, we end this report with a number of suggestions for moving society forward in a more positive direction towards the next generation.

Final thoughts

The emergence of schools as institutions explicitly connected to socialisation through the direct transmission of values and political viewpoints has occurred with little public discussion. Similarly, there has been little national debate about whether it is the role of parents or teachers to make decisions on issues such as the contents of a packed lunch, the correct age to walk home alone, or when it is appropriate to learn about sex and relationships. A first step in restoring adult authority is taking this conversation to the public.

An important requirement for this national conversation is clearer communication between school and home. The Department for Education has clarified that schools 'can and should share relationships, sex and health education curriculum materials with parents' and that parents should 'have confidence in their right to know what children are seeing and being taught in the classroom.'[131] Under new government guidance, teachers should also inform parents if their child wishes to change their gender identity at school.[132] But the fact that such guidance is necessary reveals the breakdown in communication between school and home and the extent to which schools have assumed the right to act on behalf of the child without the knowledge or consent of parents. It is vital that, despite a change of government, this guidance remains in place.

There needs to be a far clearer demarcation of responsibilities between school and home. For example, it is the job of parents, not school teachers, to ensure that children can use a toilet. If children are still wearing nappies on a routine basis then they are not ready for school. Likewise, it is the responsibility of parents, not teachers, to shape children's attitudes to gender identity and sexuality. The primary role of the school is the transmission of knowledge and the primary role of the family is nurturing children, including their moral and spiritual development.

Restoring collective adult authority means removing the institutionalisation of ungrounded suspicion from adults who volunteer to help with community projects such as youth clubs, scouts or guides, or grandparents who volunteer to hear primary school children read. The need for formal clearance from the Disclosure and Barring Service for anyone who has contact with children may have been initially well intentioned but an obsessive focus on paperwork rather than instinct can cause more problems than it solves.

Post Covid lockdowns, state institutions need to re-state their commitment to parents and children. There needs to be clear recognition that the blanket closure of schools, health services and childcare provision was scientifically unjustifiable and morally wrong. Parents need reassurance that services will not be withdrawn in the future without clear evidence that there is no alternative and even then any closures must be for a strictly time-limited period.

Teachers need to be reminded of the important role they play in relation to the transmission of knowledge, and, through this, cultural norms and values. Teachers should be rewarded and respected for high levels of subject expertise more than for a general interest in the wellbeing of children. Similarly, we need greater cultural validation for the institution of the family. Not all families exist in circumstances that parenting experts consider ideal. However, what matters more than either specific circumstances or diligence in following official guidance is that the overwhelming majority of parents love their children and want what is best for them.

Notes

1   Williams, J. (2024) 'In defence of Katharine Birbalsingh' in *Spiked* (19/01/24). Available at: https://www.spiked-online.com/2024/01/19/in-defence-of-katharine-birbalsingh/ (Accessed 12/03/24).

2   Andrews, M. (2023) 'Challenge of Reception class children still in the nappy years' in *Shropshire Star* (27/01/23). Available at: https://www.shropshirestar.com/news/education/2023/01/27/challenge-of-reception-children-still-in-the-nappy-years/ (Accessed 05/02/24).

3   Safe Schools Alliance UK (2021) Advice on social transitioning of trans-identified children. Available at: https://safeschoolsallianceuk.net/wp-content/uploads/2021/08/22Aug_Advice-note-schools-socially-transitioning.pdf (Accessed 05/02/24).

4   Clarence-Smith, L. (2023) 'Schools block parents from seeing 'harmful' sex education materials' in *The Telegraph* (23/01/23). Available at: https://safeschoolsallianceuk.net/wp-content/uploads/2021/08/22Aug_Advice-note-schools-socially-transitioning.pdf (Accessed 05/02/24).

5   Clarence-Smith, L. (2023) 'Ofsted chief's warning over explicit sex education lessons' in *The Telegraph* (09/03/23). Available at: https://www.telegraph.co.uk/news/2023/03/09/ofsted-chiefs-warning-explicit-sex-education-lessons/ (Accessed 05/02/24).

6   Kaufmann, E. (2022) 'The Political Culture of Young Britain' *Policy Exchange*. Available at: https://policyexchange.org.uk/publication/the-political-culture-of-young-britain/ (Accessed 05//02/24).

7   Department for Education (2024) "New RSHE guidance: What it means for sex education lessons in schools". Available at: https://educationhub.blog.gov.uk/2024/05/16/new-rshe-guidance-what-it-means-for-sex-education-lessons-in-schools/ (Accessed 29th July 2024).

8   United Nations Educational, Scientific and Cultural Organization (2018) *International technical guidance on sexuality education, An evidence informed approach* (Revised Edition). P. 16. Available at: https://unesdoc.unesco.org/ark:/48223/pf0000260770 (Accessed 30/01/24).

9   Department for Education (2023) What do children and young people learn in relationship, sex and health education. *The Education Hub*. Gov.UK. (10/03/23). Available at: https://educationhub.blog.gov.uk/2023/03/10/what-do-children-and-young-people-learn-in-relationship-sex-and-health-education/ (Accessed 05/02/24).

10   Malvern, J. (2023) 'Woman loses fight to make daughter's sex education content public' in *The Times* (12/06/23). Available at: https://www.thetimes.co.uk/article/woman-loses-fight-to-see-daughters-sex-education-content-3j8cg9kkt. (Accessed 29/01/24).

11   Gov.Uk. (2024) 'Age limits introduced to protect children in RSHE'. (16/05/24). Available at: https://www.gov.uk/government/news/age-limits-introduced-to-protect-children-in-rshe. (Accessed 26/07/24).

12   New Social Covenant Unit (2023) What is being taught in Relationships and Sex Education in our schools? Available at: https://www.newsocialcovenant.co.uk/wp-content/uploads/2023/08/nscu-education-2023-v1.pdf (Accessed 29/01/24).

13   Williams, J. (2023) 'The trouble with sex education' in *The Spectator*. Available at: https://www.spectator.co.uk/article/a-review-of-sex-education-in-schools-cannot-come-soon-enough/ (Accessed 29/01/24).

14   Department for Education (2023) 'Sex education: What is RSHE and can parents access curriculum materials?' on *The Education Hub*. (24/10/23). Available at: https://educationhub.blog.gov.uk/2023/10/24/rshe-relationships-health-sex-education-review-curriculum-to-protect-children/ (Accessed 05/02/24).

15   Williams, J. (2023) The trouble with sex education in *The Spectator*. (16/03/23). Available at:https://www.spectator.co.uk/article/a-review-of-sex-education-in-schools-cannot-come-soon-enough/. (Accessed 05/02/24).

16   The Advisory Group for Citizenship Report (1998) 'The Crick Report'. Available at: https://www.teachingcitizenship.org.uk/resource/advisory-group-citizenship-report-crick-report

17   Ibid

18   James Arthur, Ian Davies, Carole Hahn (eds) (2008) SAGE Handbook of Education for Citizenship and Democracy. SAGE.

19   Department for Education (2013) Citizenship programmes of study: key stages 3 and 4 National curriculum in England. (September 2013). Available at: https://assets.publishing.service.gov.uk/media/5f324f7ad3bf7f1b1ea28dca/SECONDARY_national_curriculum_-_Citizenship.pdf (Accessed 12/03/24).

20   Lundie, D. (2016) 'What to make of 'British values' in the aftermath of Brexit? In *Schools Week* (27/07/16). Available at: https://schoolsweek.co.uk/what-to-make-of-british-values-in-the-aftermath-of-brexit/

21   Selmes, I. (2019) 'Whatever happened to sustainable development?' in *Teaching Geography*, Vol. 44, No. 3 (Autumn 2019) Pp. 108-110.

22 Counsell C. (2021) 'History' in Alka Sehgal Cuthbert, Alex Standish (eds) *What Should Schools Teach?: Disciplines, subjects and the pursuit of truth (Knowledge and the Curriculum)*. UCL Press.

23 Ibid

24 For a more detailed discussion of this point, see: Kurti, P. (2022) 'Raging against the past: Guilt, justice, and the postcolonial reformation', Centre for Independent Studies, Analysis Paper 35 (April 2022).

25 Boffey, D. (2013) 'Historians attack Michael Gove over 'narrow' curriculum' in *The Guardian* (16/02/13) Available at: https://www.theguardian.com/politics/2013/feb/16/historians-michael-gove-curriculum

26 University of Oxford (2021) 'History teaching has substantially changed to address diversity, say teachers (22/10/21) Available at: https://www.ox.ac.uk/news/2021-10-22-history-teaching-has-substantially-changed-address-diversity-say-teachers

27 Somerville, E. (03/07/21) 'Decolonise your desks, demands teaching union in 'sinister' new escalation of culture wars.' in *The Telegraph*.

28 Griffiths, S. (25/04/21) "We're girls, not guys: pupils urged to protest against 'sexist' language." in *Sunday Times*.

29 Bannerman, L. (19/06/21) "St Paul's Girls' School ditches 'binary' head girl." in *The Times*.

30 London Play (2021) 'Children today have two years less freedom than their parents' Available at: https://londonplay.org.uk/our_news/45851/. (Accessed 12/03/24).

31 Haidt, J. and Paresky, P. (2015) 'By mollycoddling our children, we're fuelling mental illness in teenagers' in *The Guardian* (10/01/19). Available at: https://www.theguardian.com/commentisfree/2019/jan/10/by-mollycoddling-our-children-were-fuelling-mental-illness-in-teenagers. (Accessed 12/03/24).

32 Kildwick CE VC Primary School. Walking home alone policy. Available at: https://www.kildwickceschool.org.uk/parents/consent-forms/walking-home-alone-policy (Accessed 12/03/24).

33 Kildwick CE VC Primary School. Walking home alone policy. Available at: https://www.kildwickceschool.org.uk/parents/consent-forms/walking-home-alone-policy (Accessed 12/03/24).

34 Gov. UK National Statistics (2023) *National Travel Survey 2022: Travel to and from school*. Available at: https://www.gov.uk/government/statistics/national-travel-survey-2022/national-travel-survey-2022-travel-to-and-from-school. (Accessed 12/03/24).

35 Kildwick CE VC Primary School. Walking home alone policy. Available at: https://www.kildwickceschool.org.uk/parents/consent-forms/walking-home-alone-policy (Accessed 12/03/24).

36 Gov. UK (2023) *School Food Standards Practical Guide*. Available at: https://www.gov.uk/government/publications/school-food-standards-resources-for-schools/school-food-standards-practical-guide. (Accessed 30/07/24).

37 Gov.UK (2023) Creating a culture and ethos of healthy eating. Available at: https://www.gov.uk/government/publications/school-food-standards-resources-for-schools/creating-a-culture-and-ethos-of-healthy-eating. (Accessed 30/07/24).

38 Ibid.

39 Brighton and Hove City Council. Public Health Schools Programme. 'Packed Lunch Policy Guidance'. Available at: https://www.brighton-hove.gov.uk/sites/default/files/migrated/article/inline/School%20Lunch%20Box%20Policy_0.pdf. (Accessed 30/07/24).

40 St Winifred's Catholic Primary School. Packed Lunch Policy. Available at: https://www.swcps.lewisham.sch.uk/parents/dinner-time/packed-lunch-policy/. (Accessed 12/03/24).

41 Wibsey Primary School. Good Practice Packed Lunch Guidelines. Available at: https://wibseyprimary.co.uk/wp-content/uploads/2017/03/WPS-Good-Practice-Packed-Lunch-Guidelines-June-16.pdf (Accessed 12/03/24).

42 Crerar, P. and S. Weale (2024) 'Starmer to embrace nanny state with plans for toothbrushing in schools' in *The Guardian* (10/01/24). Available at: https://www.theguardian.com/society/2024/jan/10/keir-starmer-announces-plan-for-supervised-toothbrushing-in-schools. (Accessed 26/07/24).

43 Gov.UK Guidance. (2024) Promoting and supporting mental health and wellbeing in schools and colleges. Available at: https://www.gov.uk/guidance/mental-health-and-wellbeing-support-in-schools-and-colleges. (Accessed 12/03/24).

44 See for example https://mindfulnessinschools.org/ (Accessed 12/03/24).

45 See for example https://www.woodlandsinfantschool.co.uk/guided-meditation/ (Accessed 12/03/24).

46 See for example https://www.yogaatschool.org.uk/ (Accessed 12/03/24).

47 See for example https://mentallyhealthyschools.org.uk/getting-started/social-and-emotional-skills/ (Accessed 12/03/24).

48 St James Primary School, Social, Emotional, Mental Health and Wellbeing. Available at https://www.stjames-primary.com/home/inclusion/mental-health-and-wellbeing/ (Accessed 12/03/24).

49 Lewis, J. (2024) 'British parents have forgotten their most basic responsibilities' in *The Telegraph* (29/02/24). Available at: https://www.telegraph.co.uk/news/2024/02/29/british-parents-have-forgotten-their-most-basic-responsibil/ (Accessed 08/04/24).

50 Nutt, J. (2018) 'Teachers shouldn't have to do the parents' job, too' in *Times Educational Supplement*. (22/04/18). Available at: https://www.tes.com/magazine/archive/teachers-shouldnt-have-do-parents-job-too. (Accessed 08/04/24).

51 NASUWT (2023) *Behaviour in Schools*. (September 2023). Available at: https://www.nasuwt.org.uk/static/357990da-90f7-4ca4-b63fc3f781c4d851/Behaviour-in-Schools-Full-Report-September-2023.pdf. (Accessed 08/04/24).

52 Williams, J. (2018) "It Just Grinds You Down" *Policy Exchange*. Available at: https://policyexchange.org.uk/wp-content/uploads/2019/01/It-Just-Grinds-You-Down-Joanna-Williams-Policy-Exchange-December-2018.pdf (Accessed 08/04/24).

53 Moss, L. and Dunkley, E. (2024) 'Pupil behaviour 'getting worse' at schools in England, say teachers' in *BBC News* (28/03/24). Available at: https://www.bbc.co.uk/news/education-68674568 (Accessed 08/04/24).

54 Tominey, C. (2024). 'It's no wonder children are so badly behaved. Just look at their parents.' in *The Telegraph* (10/01/24). Available at: https://www.telegraph.co.uk/news/2024/01/19/no-wonder-children-are-so-badly-behaved-look-at-parents/ (Accessed 08/04/24).

55 Anna Freud. Mentally Healthy Schools. Home Environment. Available at: https://mentallyhealthyschools.org.uk/factors-that-impact-mental-health/home-based-risk-factors/home-environment/# (Accessed 08/04/24).

56 BBC News. (2024) 'Batley Grammar School protest report 'deeply disturbing' – MP' (26/03/24). Available at: https://www.bbc.co.uk/news/uk-england-leeds-68659435 (Accessed 08/04/24).

57 James, R. and Goss, L. (2023) 'Parents and school at war over 'strict' rules' in *The Mail*. (21/09/23) Available at: https://www.dailymail.co.uk/news/article-12545475/Parents-school-war-Mother-says-daughter-refuses-drink-lessons-doesnt-fall-victim-new-toilet-break-crackdown-head-blames-mums-dads-whipping-unrest-Facebook-police-called-protest.html (Accessed 08/04/23).

58 Education Policy Institute (2023) 'Examining post-pandemic absences in England' (19/05/23). Available at: https://epi.org.uk/publications-and-research/absence/# (Accessed 09/04/24).

59 Children's Commissioner (2024) 'New figures reveal drop in number of school absences, but attendance must remain top priority' (25/01/24). Available at: https://www.childrenscommissioner.gov.uk/blog/new-figures-reveal-drop-in-number-of-school-absences/ (Accessed 09/04/24).

60 Weale, S. (2023) 'Parents in England no longer see daily school attendance as vital, report finds' in *The Guardian* (21/09/23). Available at: https://www.theguardian.com/education/2023/sep/21/parents-in-england-no-longer-see-daily-school-attendance-as-vital-report-finds (Accessed 09/04/24).

61 Macmillan, L. and Anders, J. (2024) 'Rising school absence: what do we know and what can we do?' in IOE Blog, UCL. (16/01/24). Available at: https://blogs.ucl.ac.uk/ioe/2024/01/16/rising-school-absence-what-do-we-know-and-what-can-we-do/ (Accessed 09/04/24).

62 Hussey, J. (2024) 'Working from home has ruined school attendance – I've seen it happen first-hand' in *The Telegraph* (11/01/24). Available at: https://www.telegraph.co.uk/education-and-careers/2024/01/11/work-from-home-impact-school-attendance/# (Accessed 09/04/24).

63 Brown, G. (2024) 'Reception pupils in nappies reveals societal challenges' in *TES* (03/03/24). Available at: https://www.tes.com/magazine/analysis/early-years/reception-pupils-nappies-shows-school-ready-problem-society (Accessed 08/04/24).

64 Weale, S. (2024) 'One in four school-starters in England and Wales not toilet-trained, say teachers' in *The Guardian* (28/02/24). Available at: https://www.theguardian.com/education/2024/feb/28/one-in-four-school-starters-in-england-and-wales-not-toilet-trained-say-teachers# (Accessed 08/04/24).

65 Ibid.

66 Bell, D. (2024) 'Pandemic babies are arriving at school still wearing nappies. Where's the plan to help them?' in *The Guardian* (05/01/24). Available at: https://www.theguardian.com/commentisfree/2024/jan/05/children-school-early-years-education-pandemic-covid (Accessed 08/04/24).

67 Busby, E. (2018) 'Parents too busy to teach children how to use toilet before starting school, suggests Ofsted boss' in *The Independent* (01/06/18). Available at: https://www.independent.co.uk/news/education/education-news/parents-ofsted-amanda-spielman-nursery-children-toilet-potty-a8379046.html (Accessed 17/04/24).

68   Nuffield Foundation. (2020) 'Lives of the under-fives strikingly
     different from a generation ago' (26/11/20). Available at: https://
     www.nuffieldfoundation.org/news/lives-of-under-fives-strikingly-
     different-today. (Accessed 26/07/24).

69   See, for example, healthychildren.org 'Emotional Growth Needed
     for Toilet Training' Available at: https://www.healthychildren.
     org/English/ages-stages/toddler/toilet-training/Pages/Emotional-
     Growth-Needed-For-Toilet-Training.aspx (Accessed 17/04/24).

70   Weale, S. (2024) 'One in four school-starters in England and Wales
     not toilet-trained, say teachers' in *The Guardian* (28/02/24). Available
     at: https://www.theguardian.com/education/2024/feb/28/one-in-
     four-school-starters-in-england-and-wales-not-toilet-trained-say-
     teachers# (Accessed 08/04/24).

71   Oakeshott, M. (2001) *The Voice of Liberal Learning*. Indianapolis:
     Liberty Fund. p. 91

72   Oakeshott, M. (2001) *The Voice of Liberal Learning*. Indianapolis:
     Liberty Fund. p. 10

73   In Lee, E., Bristow, J., Faircloth, C. and Macvarish, J. (2023) *Parenting
     Culture Studies*. London: Palgrave Macmillan. Page 7

74   Lasch, C. (1977) *Haven in a Heartless World*. London: W.W. Norton
     and Company. p. Xx

75   PA Media. (2024) 'Proportion of married people in England and
     Wales falls below 50% for first time' in *The Guardian* (29/01/24).
     Available at: https://www.theguardian.com/lifeandstyle/2024/jan/25/
     proportion-of-married-people-in-england-and-wales-falls-below-50-
     for-first-time# (Accessed 14/06/24).

76   Statista. (2024) 'Number of live births in England and Wales from
     2000 to 2021, by marital status of mother'. Available at: https://www.
     statista.com/statistics/294571/live-births-in-england-wales-uk-by-
     age-and-marital-status-of-mother/# (Accessed 14/06/24).

77   Bloom, J. (2024) 'How should countries deal with falling birth rates?'
     at *BBC News* (20/05/24). Available at: https://www.bbc.co.uk/news/
     articles/c72p2vgd21no# (Accessed 14/06/24).

78   Furedi, F. (2009) *Wasted: Why Education Isn't Educating*. London:
     Continuum. p. 113

79   Lee, E., Bristow, J., Faircloth, C. and Macvarish, J. (2023) *Parenting
     Culture Studies*. London: Palgrave Macmillan. Page 116.

80   Lee, E., Bristow, J., Faircloth, C. and Macvarish, J. (2023) *Parenting
     Culture Studies*. London: Palgrave Macmillan. Page 126.

81   Furedi, F. (2009) *Wasted: Why Education Isn't Educating*. London:
     Continuum. p. 92

82   Brigitte Berger (2002) *The Family in the Modern Age More than a lifestyle choice*. London: Transaction Publishers. p. 8

83   Brigitte Berger (2002) *The Family in the Modern Age More than a lifestyle choice*. London: Transaction Publishers. p. 91

84   Furedi, F. (2009) *Wasted: Why Education Isn't Educating*. London: Continuum. p. 98

85   Lee, E., Bristow, J., Faircloth, C. and Macvarish, J. (2023) *Parenting Culture Studies*. London: Palgrave Macmillan. Page 27.

86   Furedi, F. (2009) *Wasted: Why Education Isn't Educating*. London: Continuum. p. 106

87   BBC News. (2019) 'Named person scheme scrapped by Scottish government' (19/09/19). Available at: https://www.bbc.co.uk/news/uk-scotland-scotland-politics-49753980. (Accessed 14/06/24).

88   Lee, E., Bristow, J., Faircloth, C. and Macvarish, J. (2023) *Parenting Culture Studies*. London: Palgrave Macmillan. Page 127

89   Lee, E., Bristow, J., Faircloth, C. and Macvarish, J. (2023) *Parenting Culture Studies*. London: Palgrave Macmillan. Page 19

90   Lee, E., Bristow, J., Faircloth, C. and Macvarish, J. (2023) *Parenting Culture Studies*. London: Palgrave Macmillan. Page 24

91   Lee, E., Bristow, J., Faircloth, C. and Macvarish, J. (2023) *Parenting Culture Studies*. London: Palgrave Macmillan. Page 61

92   Furedi, F. (2009) *Wasted Why Education Isn't Educating*. London: Continuum. p. 104

93   Larkin, P. (1971) 'This be the verse'. Poetry Foundation. Available at: *https://www.poetryfoundation.org/poems/48419/this-be-the-verse*. (Accessed 26/07/24).

94   Brigitte Berger (2002) *The Family in the Modern Age More than a lifestyle choice*. London: Transaction Publishers. p. ?

95   Lee, E., Bristow, J., Faircloth, C. and Macvarish, J. (2023) *Parenting Culture Studies*. London: Palgrave Macmillan. Page 18

96   Furedi, F. (2009) *Wasted: Why Education Isn't Educating*. London: Continuum. p. 96

97   Lee, E., Bristow, J., Faircloth, C. and Macvarish, J. (2023) *Parenting Culture Studies*. London: Palgrave Macmillan. Page 5

98   Frawley, A. (2024) Significant Emotions Rhetoric and Social Problems in a Vulnerable Age. London: Bloomsbury p. 66

99   Brigitte Berger (2002) *The Family in the Modern Age More than a lifestyle choice*. London: Transaction Publishers. p. 11

100 Sophie Lewis, Abolish the Family, page 14

101 Sophie Lewis, Abolish the Family, page 15

102 Frawley, A. (2024) Families in Fragments. MCC Brussels. Available at: https://brussels.mcc.hu/uploads/default/0001/01/d199e23aed7ff0436fbc88c46081ce716fd2687a.pdf. (Accessed 14/06/24).

103 Brigitte Berger (2002) *The Family in the Modern Age More than a lifestyle choice.* London: Transaction Publishers. p. 58

104 Oakeshott, M. (2001) *The Voice of Liberal Learning.* Indianapolis: Liberty Fund. p. 10

105 Dewey, J. (2018). *Democracy and Education* [Kindle iOS version].

106 Dewey, J. (2018). *Democracy and Education* [Kindle iOS version].

107 Dewey, J. (2018). *Democracy and Education* [Kindle iOS version].

108 Arendt, A. (1954) The Crisis in Education. Available at: https://thi.ucsc.edu/wp-content/uploads/2016/09/Arendt-Crisis_In_Education-1954.pdf. (Accessed 26/07/24).

109 In Furedi, F. (2009) *Wasted: Why Education Isn't Educating.* London: Continuum. p. 90

110 Furedi, F. (2009) *Wasted: Why Education Isn't Educating.* London: Continuum. p. 88

111 Hirsch, E. D. (2017) *Why Knowledge Matters.* Cambridge, Massachusetts: Harvard Education Press. p. 198

112 Hirsch, E. D. (2017) *Why Knowledge Matters.* Cambridge, Massachusetts: Harvard Education Press. p. 195

113 Hirsch, E. D. (2017) *Why Knowledge Matters.* Cambridge, Massachusetts: Harvard Education Press. p. 195

114 Hirsch, E. D. (2017) *Why Knowledge Matters.* Cambridge, Massachusetts: Harvard Education Press. p. 185

115 Furedi, F. (2009) *Wasted: Why Education Isn't Educating.* London: Continuum. p. 92

116 Dewey, J. (2018). *Democracy and Education* [Kindle iOS version].

117 Dewey, J. (2018). *Democracy and Education* [Kindle iOS version].

118 George S. Counts. (1932) Dare The School Build A New Social Order? New York: The John Day Company P. 37

119 George S. Counts. (1932) Dare The School Build A New Social Order? New York: The John Day Company P. 3

120 Arendt, A. (1954) The Crisis in Education. Available at: https://thi.ucsc.edu/wp-content/uploads/2016/09/Arendt-Crisis_In_Education-1954.pdf. (Accessed 26/07/24).

121 George S. Counts. (1932) Dare The School Build A New Social Order? New York: The John Day Company P. 19

122 Oakeshott, M. (2001) *The Voice of Liberal Learning.* Indianapolis: Liberty Fund. p. 104

123 Oakeshott, M. (2001) *The Voice of Liberal Learning*. Indianapolis: Liberty Fund. p. 99

124 Furedi, F. (2009) *Wasted: Why Education Isn't Educating*. London: Continuum. p. 83

125 Furedi, F. (2009) *Wasted Why Education Isn't Educating*. London: Continuum. p. 89

126 Furedi, F. (2009) *Wasted Why Education Isn't Educating*. London: Continuum. p. 98

127 Francis, S. (2024) 'I'm up for fight over nanny state accusations, says Keir Starmer' at BBC News. (11/01/24). Available at: https://www.bbc.co.uk/news/uk-politics-67943548. (Accessed 18/06/24).

128 Lee, E., Bristow, J., Faircloth, C. and Macvarish, J. (2023) *Parenting Culture Studies*. London: Palgrave Macmillan. P. 23

129 Gov.UK (2024) Pupil attendance in schools. (13/06/24). Available at: https://explore-education-statistics.service.gov.uk/find-statistics/pupil-attendance-in-schools. (Accessed 18/06/24).

130 Lee, E., Bristow, J., Faircloth, C. and Macvarish, J. (2023) *Parenting Culture Studies*. London: Palgrave Macmillan. P. 427

131 Education Secretary says parents can see sex education material – GOV.UK (www.gov.uk)

132 https://www.bbc.co.uk/news/uk-67754359

CIVITAS

Our Aims and Programmes
- We facilitate informed public debate by providing accurate factual information on the social issues of the day, publishing informed comment and analysis, and bringing together leading protagonists in open discussion. Civitas never takes a corporate view on any of the issues tackled during the course of this work. Our current focus is on issues such as education, health, crime, social security, manufacturing, the abuse of human rights law, and the European Union.

- We ensure that there is strong evidence for all our conclusions and present the evidence in a balanced and objective way. Our publications are usually refereed by independent commentators, who may be academics or experts in their field.

- We strive to benefit public debate through independent research, reasoned argument, lucid explanation and open discussion. We stand apart from party politics and transitory intellectual fashions.

- Uniquely among think tanks, we play an active, practical part in rebuilding civil society by running schools on Saturdays and after-school hours so that children who are falling behind at school can achieve their full potential.

Subscriptions and Membership (UK only)
If you would like to stay abreast of Civitas' latest work, you can have all of our books delivered to your door as soon as they are published. New subscribers receive a free copy of Roger Bootle's book, *The AI Economy: Work, Wealth and Welfare in the Robot Age* and Daniel Bentley's book, *The Land Question* on fixing the dysfunction at the root of the housing crisis. For those who would like to support our work further and get involved in our Westminster events, we have a variety of Subscription and Membership options available:
https://www.civitasonline.org.uk/product-category/subscriptions/

We regret that we are unable to post items to non-UK residents, although all of our publications are individually available via our Civitas Book Store (https://www.civitasonline.org.uk) and in most cases on Amazon.

Renewals for Existing Members

If you are an existing member wishing to renew with ease and convenience, please do select one of the subscription or membership options that most closely meets your requirements.

Make a Donation

If you like our work and would like to help see it continue, please consider making a donation. A contribution of any amount, big or small, will help us advance our research and educational activities. You can make a donation by getting in touch (020 7799 6677) or sending a simple email to info@civitas.org.uk so that we can come back to you.

Supporters of Civitas

Because we want to reach as wide an audience as possible, our subscription and membership fees are set as low as possible and barely meet printing and postage expenses. To meet the costs of producing our research and conducting our educational projects, we rely entirely on the goodwill and generosity of people who value our work.

If you would like to support our work on a rolling basis, there is a variety of advanced membership levels on offer. Supporters of Civitas have the opportunity to become more deeply engaged with the work their philanthropy makes possible.

You can pay by selecting a membership or subscription option and we will be in contact.

Alternatively, just call us on +44 (0)20 7799 6677 or email info@civitas.org.uk and we can discuss your options.

If it is your preference, please make cheques payable to Civitas.

Civitas: Institute for the Study of Civil Society
First Floor
55 Tufton Street
Westminster
London
SW1P 3QL

Email: subs@civitas.org.uk